# *Louder Than Words*

# LOUDER
## *than* WORDS

## ANDY STANLEY

Multnomah® Publishers *Sisters, Oregon*

LOUDER THAN WORDS
published by Multnomah Publishers, Inc.

© 2004 by Andy Stanley
International Standard Book Number: 1-59052-346-6

Cover design by David Carlson Design

Unless otherwise indicated, Scripture quotations are from:
*New American Standard Bible*
© 1960, 1977 by the Lockman Foundation

Other Scripture quotations are from:
*The Holy Bible,* New International Version (NIV) © 1973, 1984 by International Bible Society,
used by permission of Zondervan Publishing House.
*The Holy Bible,* New King James Version (NKJV) © 1984 by Thomas Nelson, Inc.

*Multnomah* is a trademark of Multnomah Publishers, Inc.,
and is registered in the U.S. Patent and Trademark Office.
The colophon is a trademark of Multnomah Publishers, Inc.

Printed in the United States of America

For information:
MULTNOMAH PUBLISHERS, INC.
POST OFFICE BOX 1720
SISTERS, OREGON 97759

Library of Congress Cataloging-in-Publication Data

Stanley, Andy.
  Louder than words / by Andy Stanley.
      p. cm.
  ISBN 1-59052-346-6 (pbk.)
  1. Christian life. 2. Character—Religious aspects—Christianity.  I. Title.
  BV4599.5.C45S73 2004
  248.4—dc22

                              2003025209

04 05 06 07 08 09 10—10 9 8 7 6 5 4 3 2 1 0

For Sandra,
the finest woman I know.

# Contents

# FOREWORD

Undeniably, character is the foundation of all true leadership. The apostle Paul placed such emphasis on unblemished character that he listed it as the first qualification for Christian leadership: "An overseer, then, must be above reproach" (1 Timothy 3:2). Out of character great leaders such as Winston Churchill and Billy Graham have been born. And out of a life of character has this book been born.

For quite a while I've watched Andy Stanley grow as a leader and pastor. In the past couple of years, I've gotten to know him well. The more I see, the better I like him. And I can say without a doubt that he lives out the solid character principles that he shares in this book.

*Louder Than Words* will lead you through the process of discovering things about your beliefs and your values. The impact of a personal value system is comprehensive, encompassing everything in our lives from professional achievement to the way we relate to our children and spouses. And it affects that most important of relationships—the one we have with God.

Step by step, you will be encouraged to target specific character qualities and to discover your true values. You will learn to evaluate your relationships, occupational goals, and even entertainment in the light of character issues. And you will discover whether your goals are character-oriented or achievement-oriented. You will uncover obstacles to personal character development that you did not realize existed. You will also learn to accept responsibility for your own deficiencies. Most important, *Louder Than Words* provides you with specific strategies for change, strategies that will help you to develop unwavering character.

This world desperately needs people of vision and personal conviction. It needs mothers and fathers, employees and managers, citizens and officials who will do what is right regardless of the personal cost. It needs people who are willing to become more like Christ and lead by example. *Louder Than Words* can help you become such a person.

*John C. Maxwell*
Founder, The INJOY Group

# MY DAD, MY HERO

I was thirteen when I learned the meaning of the phrase "Actions speak louder than words." My dad was an associate pastor at First Baptist Church of Atlanta when the senior pastor resigned under pressure from the board of deacons. While a search was conducted for a fitting replacement, my father was asked to "fill the pulpit." That's church talk for "preach on Sundays."

Well, fill it he did. And not only did he fill the pulpit, he started filling the pews as well. Young families started returning to the church in record numbers. The youth ministry began to grow. Volunteerism was at an all-time high. Everybody was excited about the new energy that radiated from this historic downtown church.

Well, almost everybody.

As is the case in too many churches, there was a group of men and women who had been around longer than everybody else and felt as if the church somehow belonged to them. After all, it was their money that paid for most of the new chapel. And apart from their influence, the city may have never allowed the church to build the gymnasium. These people chaired all the key committees, including the committee on committees that determined who served on the committees. They were the *they* of First Baptist Atlanta. And *they* did not appreciate my dad's sudden popularity or the influence it gave him with the membership.

To make matters worse, there was a grassroots movement afoot to elect my dad as senior pastor. And why not? He was a phenomenal communicator. He demonstrated great leadership ability. And he had a vision for the church. What more could a congregation ask for? Depends on who you were asking.

The power people thought he was too young (he was forty), too evangelistic (he invited people to come forward at the end of services), and too mystical. By "mystical" they meant that he preached openly about a personal relationship with God. He also had the nerve to challenge the congregation to pray for God's will concerning the future of the church. Now *that* was a real problem. Before that time the power people simply got together and decided the future of the church; the notion of seeking God's will on the matter was completely foreign to them.

Bottom line, *they* knew they would not be able to control Dad. So they had but one choice: Get rid of him. At first they asked nicely for him to step down. Then they bribed him. Eventually the bribes turned to threats. Not made-for-primetime, *CNN Presents*–type threats. *They* were more subtle than that.

My dad's response to all of this marked me for life. The way he saw it, God had brought him to that place. And when God told him to leave, he would load us all up in the Grand Safari station wagon and we would go. There were times when he asked God for permission to leave, but he always received the same answer: *Stay where you are. Keep doing what you are doing.* Dad was very up-front with the group that wanted him gone. He assured them that if the congregation voted him out, he would leave quietly. That would be his assurance that God had another ministry assignment for him elsewhere.

Well, things continued to heat up. The power brokers started taking members of the congregation to dinner. People started taking sides. Nasty things were said, anonymous letters written and distributed. It was church politics at their worst. Yet in spite of all that, the church continued to grow and prosper.

Then the church meeting to end all church meetings took place.

It was about two weeks before the church was scheduled to come together and vote on whether or not to allow my dad to continue in his role as associate pastor. I was sitting about six rows back on the right during our regular Wednesday evening service. The program was just beginning when one of the deacons walked up to the pulpit to make an announcement. Deacon Myers was part of the crew committed to my dad's speedy departure.

Once "Brother" Myers finished his brief announcement, he began sharing some of his personal feelings about the brewing controversy. The longer he talked, the more angry and animated he became. Then, to everyone's horror, he used the word *damn.* I'll never forget sitting in a Baptist church in 1974 and hearing a deacon say "damn" from behind the pulpit. My dad immediately stood, walked up beside Deacon Myers, and said, "Now you need to watch your language…"

Before my dad could finish his sentence, the deacon raised a fist toward my dad's face and said, "No, you'd better watch *yourself*, or you might get punched!"

Frozen in my memory is the still picture of Deacon Myers's clenched fist poised inches away from my dad's face. I don't know exactly how long the two of them stood there, locked in eye-to-eye combat, but it seemed like an eternity. Eventually, Deacon Myers got the message: Dad wasn't going to back down. It was time for the deacon to fish or cut bait. Deacon Myers decided to fish. To the shock of everyone in the congregation—brother, sister, deacon, Sunday school teacher—Myers reared back and smacked my dad right in the jaw.

This was a defining moment for me.

As a thirteen-year-old, I saw firsthand what it looked like to do the right thing even when it cost something. I sat there and watched my hero, my dad, stand up to the forces of evil and win without firing a shot. I knew then that I wanted to be that kind of man.

But as I was to discover, there is a price to be paid to become a man of character. Integrity and courage are virtues that must be nurtured and developed over time. Desire alone is not enough.

In the pages that follow, I am going to introduce you to several exercises and principles that have been extraordinarily helpful to me in my pursuit of the kind of courage and character I saw demonstrated that night as an eighth grader. My goal in writing this book is to create a tool that will help you become a man or woman of exemplary character—a person whose commitment to do the right thing inspires others as my father's courage inspired me.

Speaking of my father...

After being hit, my dad staggered back for just a moment and then stepped back up beside Deacon Myers without saying a word. No words were necessary. In an instant my dad, Charles Stanley, had become a hero while Deacon Myers and his cohorts had been exposed. From that moment on, it didn't really matter what anybody said.

Because actions speak louder than words.

# Chapter One

# The Making of a Mountain

October 21, 1966. It was another enchanting morning in the tiny Welsh village of Aberfan. As dawn broke across the shimmering emerald valleys of South Wales, the townspeople began to stir in the slate-roofed homes that speckled the hillsides of this coal mining town. A stream of ash-coated figures flowed steadily into the colliery that had given birth to this quaint community.

Not far away, ten-year-old Dilys Powell made her way down the cobblestone streets to gather with classmates in the Pantglas Junior and Infants School on Merry Road. On a typical day, this stately red brick building was home for some two hundred and fifty children of the village.

To the weathered men and women who bore the scars of a lifetime in the coal pits, this town was not without its faults. But through the untainted eyes of a child, every scene added depth to a colorful tapestry called home. Through the dusty windowpanes along the back of the school, the verdant hills were vibrant with color. The one exception was the tall, foreboding black mountain that stood at the edge of town.

To the casual observer, it appeared as an unusually shaped monolith— a single piece of rock piercing the earth's crust and serving as the foundation for the entire region. But the people of Aberfan knew better. For them it was a monument to the years of labor that had made Aberfan home.

In the moments that followed, this same monument was to capture the attention of children and adults the world over.

Since 1870, the pile of mining debris had been rising ever so gradually from the valley floor. Huge bins, carted by overhead cables, had been dumping loads of coal waste continually for nearly a century. As the townspeople were lulled by the years of monotonous dumping, the slag heap had gradually become a natural part of the landscape. Now it stood hundreds of feet high.

October had seen abnormally heavy rains fall upon the valley, turning the coal mound and the surrounding earth into a giant sponge. On the morning of October 21, David John Evans, a maintenance worker at the local colliery, climbed the hill near the waste pile to look into reports that the giant mass was moving. Without realizing it, he had just assumed a front-row seat for one of the worst mining disasters in history.

By 9:30 A.M. Dylis Powell and her friends had taken their seats. "We were laughing and playing among ourselves, waiting for our teacher to call the register," she recalled later. "We heard a noise and the room seemed to be flying around. The desks were falling and the children were shouting and screaming."

Across the street, Mrs. Pearl Crowe heard a low rumble and glanced out her window. "I saw a black mass of moving waste pouring steadily into the school, and part of the school collapsed. I was paralyzed."

When Mrs. Gwyneth Davies heard the noise, she turned in time to see that "the mountain had covered the school."

In a matter of seconds, the face of Aberfan changed forever. Liquefied by the heavy rains, two million tons of coal, rock, and mud flowed down the mountainside and into the valley. The school, along with a cluster of homes, was crushed. More than two hundred people, mostly children, were killed. An entire generation of Aberfan had been virtually wiped out. And all because of a mountain that wasn't really a mountain at all.

For years, the people of Aberfan had worked to build a community. The giant coal mountain stood like the centerpiece of a city carved out of the Welsh landscape by years of diligent labor. It was a growing legacy left for each passing generation. But in the course of one day, all of that changed.

But this was a day that had been in the making for some time.

## ABERFAN REVISITED

As a pastor, I spend a great deal of time with people who are digging themselves out from under personal catastrophes—events that were often years in the making, but which took them "by surprise." A broken marriage, an unwanted pregnancy, a financial crisis, problems at work. As I listen, two questions race through my mind: *Why is it that we have such a difficult time recognizing the traps we lay for ourselves?* and *What could this person have done to avoid this situation?*

The answers almost always seem to boil down to the same issue.

Character.

Compromised convictions. Reshuffled values. Selfishness. Somewhere these individuals veered off the path of rightness. But nothing happened at first. At least nothing they were aware of. This was the beginning of their personal slag heap. And it stood within striking distance of their souls.

There is another group of people with whom I interface on a regular basis, those who are facing the inevitable storms of life that are not of their own making. Storms created by the character deficits of others. Storms that are a natural part of a fallen world.

There in the midst of unjust treatment and seemingly undeserved pain, the true character of a man or woman is revealed. Pretense is peeled away. Inherited, untested belief systems crumble. Religious and social correctness are jettisoned. What you see in such moments is what was really there all along.

And while many are broken, swept away by the winds of anger or despair, there emerges from the severest of storms a unique breed of people whose godly perspective and attitude remain intact. Like a great northern pine perched on an outcropping of rock, their foundations run deep. Clearly, there is more to them than meets the eye. These are the men and women who have invested years of their lives not in that which is seen, but in that which is *unseen.*

These are people of character. Men and women whose actions and attitudes speak for them. Louder than words, their lives speak of that which is within them.

## THE REAL YOU

Your character is who you truly are.

It will impact how much you accomplish in this life.

It will determine whether or not you are worth knowing.

It will make or break every one of your relationships.

Your character is instrumental in establishing how long you will be able to hold on to the fortune afforded you by hard work and good luck. Your character is the internal script that will determine your response to failure, success, mistreatment, and pain. It reaches into every single facet of your life. It is more far-reaching than your talent, your education, your background, or your network of friends. Those things can open doors for you, but your character will determine what happens once you pass through those doors.

Your good looks and net worth may get you married; your character will keep you married. Your God-given reproductive system may enable you to produce children; your character will determine your ability to relate to and communicate with those children.

This is a book about change. It's about a lifelong process of taking raw materials and molding, shaping, and refining them into a finished product. Whether you like it or not, that process is already happening inside you. It began the day you were born, and it will continue right up until the day you die.

Along the way, change is always taking place. Much of the time it goes unnoticed. Many of us planted trees as children, trees that appeared to be the same size the day we left home as they were when we planted them. Not until years later, when we returned to the old homestead, were we able to detect noticeable growth. Nevertheless, something was happening during those childhood days. A process was underway that eventually produced a mature tree. And years later we stand and marvel at the change.

What is true of every living thing is true of your character. Your character is not stagnant, but is either developing or deteriorating. You are not the same person you were yesterday. True, you may not sense any change right now. You may not be aware of any difference. But I assure you, if you were to leave and return ten years from now, you would be amazed, shocked, perhaps overjoyed, perhaps saddened at the difference.

You have changed and you are changing. And just as your outer self slowly reflects the unavoidable changes brought on by time, so your inner self takes on similar, yet not so unavoidable, changes.

## WHERE ARE YOU GOING?

Who will you be in five years? Ten years? I'm not referring to your role or job title. For just a moment, lay aside the dreams that involve your career or net worth. I'm talking about what you hope to find on the *inside*. What kind of person do you hope to become?

Today, you took a step. You either moved closer to or further away from what you hope to be. Most people moved further away. A handful overcame the negative inertia of this fallen world and moved forward. But nobody—*nobody*—stood still.

Conducting funerals is certainly not the most pleasant aspect of my job, but one thing is unmistakably clear: There are good funerals, and there are bad funerals. At a good funeral you celebrate a life—you hear stories about love, kindness, putting others first, faithfulness, mentoring, sharing. At a bad funeral you hear stories about golf and decorating.

There's certainly nothing wrong with golf or decorating. But when your assignment is to take three minutes and share with friends and family members what you remember most about Ol' So-'n'-So, and to fill the time you have to tell a golf story... Come on.

My point? Your character, not accomplishments or acquisitions, determines your legacy. Is that important? Yes, it's very important. And the older you get, the more important it will become. The problem is, character is like a tree—it doesn't develop overnight. Real character is developed over a lifetime. You can't wait until the last minute, pull an all-nighter, and expect to earn a passing grade. The measure of a man or woman's character is not determined by a fill-in-the-blank or true-or-false exam.

This is an essay test.

An essay that takes a lifetime to write.

Today you wrote a section.

It wasn't a long section. By itself it probably wasn't even a significant section. Today's section was likely only a slight variation on yesterday's. But look back in ten years—or twenty years—and you will be surprised. Whether it is a pleasant or unpleasant surprise is completely up to you.

"Hold on," you say. "Completely up to me? I don't think so. There are a lot of things that impact my character that I have no control over!"

You're right if you're talking about your starting point—where you began and who you began with. Certainly there are events, experiences, abuses that can put you at a disadvantage in the starting blocks of life. You do not choose your starting point. But you do have the opportunity—and responsibility—to choose where you end up. Because character is not as much about what you are as it is what you are *becoming*. It is not so much an issue of where you are as it is where you are headed.

One more thing. This is not a solo flight. This is not a "be all you can be" kind of thing. The truth is, most of us are being all we can be. And that's the problem. Being all we can be isn't enough. We need to be what we aren't, and, left to our own devices, we cannot become anything other than what we are.

And so our merciful heavenly Father smiles (and, in some cases, shakes His head) and offers a hand. A very large hand.

For those God foreknew he also predestined to be conformed to
the likeness of his Son…. If God is for us, who can be against us?

ROMANS 8:29, 31, NIV

Simply put, the Creator of the universe plans to be intimately involved in the process of moving your character in a positive direction. He has an agenda for your inner man, your character. That part of you that will share eternity with Him. That part of you that, more than any other, determines who you really are.

This book is a strategy for character development.

Every day of your life you go head-to-head with a master strategist. One who hates you. One who is intent on depleting your character of anything that in any way reflects the nature or fingerprint of your Father in heaven.

In this book I plan to offer you a time-tested strategy to aid in that struggle.

*Chapter Two*

# What Is Character?

*Human beings all over the earth have this curious idea
that they ought to behave in a certain way,
and they can't really get rid of it.*

C. S. Lewis

It was supposed to be the greatest achievement in the history of astronomy. It cost nearly four billion dollars and took more than six thousand men and women nearly a decade to engineer. It was respectfully named after one of the most heralded pioneers in astronomy, Dr. Edwin P. Hubble, a man who changed our understanding of the universe.

The idea was to place a highly-advanced telescope into orbit, where it could collect data from high above the distorting effects of the earth's atmosphere. Scientists would be able to gather and decipher light from a distance of more than twenty billion light years. Specialists across the country were contracted to oversee the development of thousands of vital parts. Solar panels were designed to power the twenty-five-hundred-pound telescope's delicate maneuvers. Engineers developed an intricate system of gyroscopes to maintain precise aim at objects in the endless depths of the universe.

The crowning glory was the telescope's main mirror. Over nine feet in diameter, it took six years to grind the concave masterpiece to exact specifications. The lengthy process involved polishing the optics in microscopic increments at each pass, while keeping uniform consistency across the entire width of the mirror.

Finally, on April 24, 1990, the roar of rocket engines rumbled across central Florida, announcing the launch of NASA's space shuttle *Discovery.* The shuttle astronauts would place the Hubble Space Telescope into orbit some three hundred miles above the earth. Back at the Space Telescope Science Institute in Baltimore, Maryland, crowds gathered around computer screens, waiting for the first images from the world's first orbiting observatory.

As the data began to pour in, however, the air of anticipation gradually turned into bewilderment, then to disbelief, and finally to utter shock.

The unthinkable had happened.

The lenses wouldn't focus!

Even the closest planets appeared as blurred blobs. Familiar stars were no more visible than they had been from the ground! When the details were finally sorted out, it was determined that the main mirror's specifications were off by one-fiftieth of the width of a human hair. The telescope was virtually useless.

It would require nearly four years and hundreds of millions of dollars to rectify the error. In a daring series of spacewalks, astronauts installed an elaborate system of corrective optics inside the telescope, thus redeeming one of the space program's greatest blunders.

All because of a mistake so small that only the most sensitive engineering equipment could detect it.

# FOCUSING ON CHARACTER

I was thirty years old when I discovered that my own "main mirror" was out of focus. In spite of what most would consider a successful launch, my picture of the future was a little fuzzy. I had good intentions. I was highly motivated. I was trained. But I was confused regarding my destination.

During this time of false starts and self-evaluation I arrived at the conclusion that my character development was more important than my career track. And if this was true, I had better find a definition for character—and quick.

That's when I learned there's no consensus on what it means to have character. We can all name various traits that a person with character demonstrates. *But what is it?* You know it when you see it, but how do you define it? And is a definition really necessary?

Absolutely. Here's why. Everybody agrees that character is important. It's something everyone expects from others. But without a clear definition, a target to shoot for, we are easily deceived into thinking that we are, in fact, men and women of character—and that it's everyone else who has a problem. My definition of character becomes whatever comes naturally to me, and character is what I wish I saw more of in you!

Without a definition we will simply follow our natural inclinations and criticize the natural inclinations of those who don't suit us.

In some circles, people are considered to have character if their behavior is friendly and nice. Others define character as standing up for one's beliefs. The rightness or wrongness of those beliefs is rarely questioned. The fact that a man or woman takes a stand is enough to brand him or her as an individual of character.

Bottom line, in our culture character is a moving target. It is subject to personality, mood, background, economic status, religious affiliation—

the list is endless. Consequently, just about anyone you ask will claim to be a person of character. Just don't ask them to define it.

## THE WHOLE TRUTH

The Bible presents an entirely different picture of character. It isn't a moving target. Biblical character finds its source in the nature of our Creator rather than in the behavioral patterns of man. Good character is nothing less than a reflection of the character of God. Our heavenly Father and His Son are character personified. They are not simply a picture of the real thing; they *are* the real thing. They define character by their existence.

For this reason, biblical character is something to which we find ourselves accountable. That being true, it's also something we are often tempted to ignore. And yet most will agree that the precepts and principles embodied in a Bible-based understanding of character are essential to healthy living and healthy relationships.

When we think in terms of what we want in a friend or a spouse; when we think about how we want our children to turn out; when we contemplate the things we wish we could change about our boss, we come back to the same baseline every time. We long to find in others such virtues as honesty, loyalty, self-control, faithfulness, patience, kindness. We may not want to commit to these things ourselves, but we certainly want to count on these characteristics in the people we associate with.

James Kouzes and Barry Posner surveyed nearly fifteen hundred managers from around the country in a study sponsored by the American Management Association. They asked the following open-ended question: "What values, personal traits, or characteristics do you look for and admire in your superiors?" More than two hundred and twenty-five different values, traits, and characteristics were identified. The most frequent response was "Has integrity, is truthful, is trustworthy, has character, has convictions."[1] As a society, we are certainly consistent when it comes to the kind of character we expect of others.

Time and again men and women demand behavior from one another that echoes the values and priorities of the apostles and prophets of old. Without necessarily realizing it, we long for others to model the character exemplified in our Savior. We recognize inconsistency in the people we live with. We are uninspired by the moral relativism of our culture, our national leaders, and even our modern-day "heroes." And many of us struggle with the notion that *right* is defined by whatever fits our needs at the moment, demonstrating there is greater consensus surrounding the issue of character than first meets the eye.

And yet we are still in search of a definition.

## CONSTRUCTING A DEFINITION

As a starting point, the definition of character we will use throughout this book is based upon two basic tenets of the faith:

1. God is the creator of all things.
2. You belong to Him.

God's absolute sovereignty is established in the very first words of the Bible. Because He possesses the power to create the heavens and the earth, it follows suit that nothing precedes or exceeds Him in power. God is the absolute origin of all things. Or to put it in His own words, "'To whom then will you liken Me, or to whom shall I be equal?" (Isaiah 40:25, NKJV).

In addition, as Manufacturer, He has published an extensive user's manual for us to follow, providing all the details for proper care and maintenance of His products—namely us. We can accept His instructions to be absolute. Sure, there are plenty of shade-tree mechanics out there who love to offer their advice, but nobody knows these products better than the Manufacturer.

But from the very beginning, God gave us the freedom to make choices. We have the freedom to choose good or bad, right or wrong. And wouldn't you know it, every single one of us beginning with Adam and Eve has picked bad over good, wrong over right. And these choices have eternal consequences.

But God came up with a rescue plan, a way to allow us to forgo the ultimate consequence of our sin. We simply trade in our old life and get a new one—absolutely free! Best of all, God agrees to run the new one for us and keep up the maintenance. In a sense, He maintains ownership while we get unlimited use of the new life. One participant described it this way: "For you have been bought with a price: therefore glorify God in your body" (1 Corinthians 6:20).

The problem with all of this is that "glorifying God" in our bodies requires the surrender of control. And nobody likes to surrender control, even when we know somebody else can do a better job than we can. But that's part of the deal. The degree to which we surrender control is the degree to which we will benefit in this life and the life to come. Jesus said, "Whoever desires to save [or keep] his life will lose it, but whoever loses his life for My sake will find it" (Matthew 16:25, NKJV).

The bottom line is that in order to become men and women of character, we must surrender to God's ownership.

So based on these two basic tenets—God's sovereignty and His right to ownership—character can be defined in this way:

*Character is the will to do what is right, as defined by God,*
*regardless of personal cost.*

Notice that there are two essential ingredients for character. First, character demands a commitment to do what is right in spite of what it might cost us personally. This means that when temptation clouds our thinking or doing "right" creates a temporary setback, we will have already made our decision based on a predetermined set of principles. Character involves doing what's right because it's the right thing to do.

Second, we must acknowledge that there is an absolute standard of right and wrong—one that exists independent of our own emotions, experiences, or desires. This standard is a permanent, unwavering benchmark by which we can measure our choices.

Of course, in our postmodern society, it is not popular to speak of absolutes in any sense. But as C. S. Lewis said, "Whenever you find a man who says he doesn't believe in real right or wrong, you will find the same man going back on this a moment later. He may break his promise to you, but if you try breaking one to him he'll be complaining 'It's not fair' before you can say Jack Robinson."[2]

By adopting this standard, as spelled out in God's Word, we arrive at a definition that is universal and applicable in all cultures and societies, at all times.

During World War II, missionary John Wolfinger took a stand that personifies this definition of character. Wolfinger was leading a group of about a hundred Christian converts in Borneo. When the Japanese military took control of the island, they sought to arrest the missionary and execute him. Wolfinger's followers devised a plan to hide him in the mountains until the danger passed. Wolfinger, however, reasoned that by running from his captors, he would be giving his new converts the wrong picture of God. When they urged him further, he explained that when the Japanese asked where Wolfinger was hiding, his followers would have to lie, and that was not acceptable.

So rather than risk leaving his followers with a compromised picture of God's character, Wolfinger stayed, was captured, and was executed.

Wolfinger recognized that lying, regardless of the circumstances, did not meet with God's approval. At the expense of his life, he maintained the will to do what was right.

In your pursuit of character, the temptation will be to adopt a definition which lacks one or both of the two key ingredients. The world encourages us to ignore the notion of an absolute system of right and wrong or, failing that, to avoid the short-term cost for adhering to it.

## ACCEPT NO SUBSTITUTES

We are created with a natural affinity to adopt some notion of character, whether it's accurate or not. And when we have not clearly defined what character is, we have a tendency to fill the void with the hollow imitations offered by the popular culture. The problem is, if you listen to a lie long enough, you will eventually believe it. Consequently, our ability to discern the difference is being stolen from us faster than you can say, "Hand me the remote." Messages fill our heads at the speed of light, and our beliefs are subtly twisted and contorted. Without knowing it, we develop a version of character that is merely a substitute, a caricature of the real thing. By failing to choose the proper definition of character, we choose to fail in the area of personal character.

Despite the fact that the entertainment industry rarely addresses the issue of character head-on, there's one glaring example worth exploring because of its bold claim to define "right" behavior. In 1989, filmmaker

Spike Lee won critical acclaim and an Oscar nomination for his movie *Do the Right Thing*.

The film depicts a day in the life of the residents of the notorious Bedford-Stuyvesant section of Brooklyn. Tensions are growing in this black ghetto area as the only prospering businesses are a Korean mini-grocery and Sal's Famous Pizzeria. Meanwhile, black businesses in the same neighborhood continue to fail. Sal, an Italian pizza chef, seems an unlikely character to become the center of a race riot, as he takes great pride in serving the locals. However, on this, "the hottest day on record," minor conflict soon reaches a boiling point. Sal's customers take issue with the fact that no African-Americans are among the photographs of celebrities that decorate Sal's Pizzeria.

Caught in the middle is Sal's delivery boy, Mookie, a black male in his twenties who feels called to stand up against racial injustice. Mookie is soon forced to choose between his loyalty to his employer and his convictions about Sal's choice of decor.

The climactic scene shows the increasingly agitated delivery boy, played by Spike Lee himself, standing in front of his place of employment and contemplating the conflict in his community. After a few moments of deliberation, he hurls a trash can through the store's front window, triggering a full-blown riot, complete with looting and fires.

The film concludes by juxtaposing quotes from Martin Luther King, Jr., and Malcolm X on the justification of violence. In the end, however, this film sends a clear message that doing "the right thing" means stirring up hatred, destroying a man's livelihood, and leveling half the city block—a position no doubt influenced by the late Malcolm X, whose civil rights mantra was "by any means necessary."

But there is a significant problem with this philosophy. As the motto focuses only on the means, all consideration of the end seems to get lost.

With no particular goal to guide him, Mookie is left to the random ideas of his own imagination. And as we will see, unless uniform principles guide our decisions, chaos results.

Believe it or not, *Do the Right Thing* is a movie about character. But as we have seen, if your definition of character is off, you miss your mark. And that's exactly what happened to Mookie in this story. His anger was understandable. From his perspective, African Americans have been suffering from centuries of persecution, from slavery to various forms of discrimination and prejudice.

The crimes against African-Americans are real and insidious. Mookie can't be blamed for wanting to see justice served. In his heart, all he wanted was to see the people of his race treated with the dignity they deserve. And in his eyes, he did the right thing. But lacking an accurate moral compass, without a proper understanding of character, his version of "the right thing" only served to deepen the rift between blacks, whites, Koreans, and Italians. His sincere attempt to do the right thing resulted in chaos. Pain. Lasting sorrow.

I see this same scenario reenacted over and over in real life. But instead of Mookie hurling a trash can through a storefront window, I see husbands and wives walking out on each other. I see children and teenagers rebelling against authority. I see employees taking advantage of employers. And in every scenario these men and women and teenagers feel justified in their actions. They sincerely feel that they are "doing the right thing." In their hearts they have an ironclad, open-and-shut case against the offending party.

If you trace it back far enough, every act of "senseless violence," whether political, racial, or domestic, begins with a genuine motive. But somewhere along the way the perpetrator, lacking an accurate moral compass, trades the genuine motive for an evil one. In this case, Mookie traded a sincere motive—the desire to see justice served—for a destructive one—revenge. And the missing link is always character. Authentic, divinely ordered, others-first character.

## THE CORE OF CHARACTER

This is an issue about which God has spoken, and He has not stuttered. Nor has He changed His mind. When we open the pages of Scripture, we discover that character is not the moving target society would have us believe. It is not a product of the "every man for himself" philosophy that prevails in our nation's capital. Neither is it defined by what passes for common practice in the marketplace. True character is defined by the very nature of Jesus Christ—a stumbling block for some, a rock-solid foundation for others.

*Character is the will to do what is right, as defined by God,*
*regardless of personal cost.*

There are a variety of other words and phrases we could use, but this will be our working definition. As we move forward, the main thing to remember is that the two basic tenets of faith shape our concept of character: (1) the belief in an absolute system of right and wrong and (2) the will to do what is right regardless of personal cost.

At the core of every character struggle is the issue of lordship. Are we willing to make Christ the Lord over our lives when it costs us personally? If not, then we'll only pay a greater price later on. It's just a matter of time. Being a person of character isn't always easy. The requirements may seem like prison walls, the guidelines like bars. That's always the case when you commit to something for which the payoff is long-term, and character is definitely a long-term proposition. But its benefits are not reserved solely for some distant, nebulous time in the future. As we are about to discover, there are benefits that can be experienced almost immediately.

# Chapter Three

# YOUR CHARACTER IS SHOWING

*Change from the inside out involves a gradual
shift away from self-protective relating
to strongly loving involvement.*

DR. LARRY CRABB

Don't look now, but your character is showing. It is especially evident to the people who know you, live with you, and work with you. These are the people who wish someone would sit you down and tell you what you either don't want to hear or can't seem to understand. These are the people who may have even attempted this from time to time. You may have looked at them and said with all sincerity, "You know, you're right—I really need to work on that." Or you politely smiled and thought, *What right do you have to tell me how to live my life?*

Like it or not, intentional or not, your character is on display to a watching world. It's really no secret. And it's showing because of the unique and unavoidable role character plays in our personal interaction.

Character is the motor oil of our relationships.

## START YOUR ENGINES

Every morning, without a second thought, hundreds of millions of people initiate one of the most intricate and elaborate marvels produced by the industrial age. The automobile engine is a quiet miracle of physics in which hundreds of complex operations are performed in a span of less than one second. This choreography of moving parts makes a military parade look like a Chinese fire drill.

And it all begins with the turn of a key.

The ignition switch makes contact, sending an electrical current snaking through a spaghetti-like network of twisted wires. Instantly, dozens of individual circuits spring to life. An electromagnet propels a whirling gear into contact with the teeth of the engine's flywheel. Immediately, the crankshaft accelerates to over three hundred revolutions per minute. A delicate timing system opens and closes valves, regulating the flow of materials through the cylinders. The first piston begins to compress the oxygen and vaporized fuel trapped in its chamber. Simultaneously, an electrical coil sends a steady charge to the distributor, which monitors the activity in each cylinder and releases a spark at the precise moment of full compression, igniting the fuel like a well-timed lightning strike. Meanwhile, the valves open in the other cylinders, releasing the exhaust and inhaling a fresh supply of oxygenated fuel. So far, approximately four-tenths of a second have elapsed.

Long before seat belts are buckled, literally hundreds of explosions will have taken place. Each one packs enough force to propel a .22-caliber bullet a distance of more than five miles. Neatly contained within the thick walls of the engine block, and muffled by a sophisticated exhaust system, these explosions are scarcely audible to the passengers.

Throughout the engine, hundreds of form-fitted metal parts begin to grind against one another as the explosions continue.

The oil pump rushes to bathe the vital components with a fresh supply of oil. In the eleven seconds it takes for the lubricant to race through the arteries of the engine and saturate the parts, the engine endures a critical transition period. During these eleven seconds, it will experience the equivalent of five hundred miles' worth of wear as its components assume an abrasive relationship with their counterparts. With only the leftover residue of oil to protect them, they wear against each other with increasing hostility.

Without oil, the same parts that were designed for such precise compatibility would destroy each other in a matter of minutes. If you don't believe me, just ignore that little red light on your dashboard!

It's not much of a stretch to see our world as a complex machine, made up of millions and millions of people interacting with each other. Uniquely positioned for specific functions, they perform individual operations vital to the efficiency of our social machine. Just as the pieces of an engine form an elaborate puzzle of interlocking parts, people interact to make society run in the form of families, friendships, businesses, marriages.

But without character, people will soon destroy one another—eventually the friction of our differences will take its toll, and individuals who seemed destined to be together will tear each other apart.

Every day, men and women who seemed perfectly suited for each other cause irreversible damage to their marriages. Compatible business associates find themselves unable to resolve petty differences. Likewise, fathers and mothers, sons and daughters, neighbors and friends watch their relationships fall completely apart over seemingly insignificant issues, while others quietly withdraw to avoid the conflict altogether.

All because of one missing ingredient: character.

Character is the lubricant that allows our personalities to mesh.

Wherever there is a deficit in character, we pay the price in our relationships. Show me two people who are madly in love and have everything in common, but who lack character, and I will show you a breakdown just waiting to happen.

Show me a good company managed by someone who lacks character, and I will show you a group of employees who find it difficult to respect their boss.

Show me a community leader who is gifted and charismatic, yet without character, and I will show you a community where conflict is inevitable.

The longer two parts interact, the greater the chance of friction between them. And the closer the relationship, it seems, the greater the potential for catastrophe. This explains why the people closest to us always seem to hurt us the most. Why husbands and wives sometimes become the bitterest of enemies. Why so many siblings grow up as classic rivals.

Sadly, however, the damage doesn't stop there. An alarming 55 percent of violent crime in America is domestic violence. Over 90 percent of murder victims are slain by someone they know. Of those, 45 percent are killed by a relative.

The closer you get to the people around you, the greater the chance that conflict will surface. Likewise, things tend to cool down when you back away. You send your bickering children to their rooms until things settle down. You storm out of the house in the middle of an argument or reach into the medicine cabinet for a few hours of temporary relief. Down the street, your neighbor has just been fired because he can't get along with his coworkers. And somewhere in your town, criminals are arrested and removed from society altogether in order to prevent further problems.

When temporary means are no longer effective, people pack their bags, call their attorneys, and give their children ultimatums. But conflict evasion won't keep the engine of society running for very long. As people are removed from key roles in the intricate machinery of relationships, it's just a matter of time before the engine begins to malfunction.

When husbands leave their wives to relieve conflict, or vice versa, the momentary relief of stress backfires on the children who face the trauma and insecurity of life without one of their parents.

When a disgruntled employee leaves his job or is fired, the resulting transition and loss of productivity is significantly taxing to the company and, eventually, to the economy in general.

And throwing our "problem" people in prison places an ever growing burden on the rest of society.

Removing ourselves from the source of friction is like removing vital parts from the intricate relational machinery—it leads to bigger problems. People are created with an inherent need for each other, whether it's meeting the utilitarian needs of daily operations or satisfying each other's personal need for intimacy. By design, we cannot thrive by avoiding our problems. They must be resolved through the liberal application of a miracle lubricant.

Character.

## A Window into Our Character

There is no clearer measure of our character than the health of our relationships. Healthy, long-term relationships are evidence of the presence of strong character. Conflict-ridden, short-term relationships are evidence of character deficiencies. Ditto for conflict-ridden, long-term relationships.

All interaction is directly affected by the character of those involved. It should come as no surprise, then, that relationships are the first things to suffer where there is a character deficit.

Promise Keepers founder Bill McCartney relayed a challenge he'd heard that had penetrated his defenses and turned his own methods of self-evaluation upside down:

> This past summer a guest speaker came to our church with a message that challenged my whole way of thinking. He began with a simple question: "Are you a man of character?" Yet it was the way he defined character that especially convicted me. He explained, "When you look into the face of a man's wife, you will see just what he is as a man. Whatever he has invested in or withheld from her is reflected in her countenance."[3]

McCartney went on to explain that when he turned to look at his wife, he saw a tired woman who had given everything to her husband's career while receiving little in return. With one glance, McCartney saw a crystal-clear reflection of his own character. Not in a mirror, but in the weary eyes of his closest companion. In that instant, he realized the powerful role character plays in our relationships.

As we subscribe to God's absolute standard of right and wrong, we are directed to focus on the needs of others instead of ourselves. Let's face it, God's character is *others*-oriented. Remember, it was "he who did not spare his own Son, but gave him up for us all" (Romans 8:32, NIV).

The pursuit of character means having a genuine concern for the people around us. It requires that we serve them, regardless of what it costs us personally. And when we take on the responsibility of looking out for the interests of those around us, it has a lubricating effect on our interactions.

## THE COMPOUNDING
## OF CHARACTER

A person who possesses character has an impact on everyone in i. sphere of influence. Men and women of character possess moral authoi. When you are with people who have proven track records in the areas of integrity and concern for others, you feel safe. You drop your guard. You may actually find yourself drawn to them. Instinctively, you may even begin emulating their approach to life and problem solving. Without meaning to, you adopt some of their standards. You follow willingly. Their character is contagious.

I'm speaking of the unique man or woman who walks away when someone begins sharing a juicy piece of gossip. It's that one-in-a-million friend who never says anything negative about you in your absence. It's the guy who quickly owns up to his mistakes instead of blaming others. It's the woman who is quick to give credit to the person who originated an idea rather than taking credit herself. It's the husband who has only positive things to say about his wife in public. It's the wife who allows her husband to lead when everyone knows she is more gifted in that area than her spouse.

There is something attractive about these kinds of people. We find ourselves wanting to be like them. We enjoy their company. Relationship with these people comes easy.

Likewise, the absence of character sets off a chain reaction of its own. When people you know have a reputation for compromising their integrity to avoid personal loss, they not only forfeit your respect, but they destroy your confidence in them as well. There is always an inner hesitancy associated with the relationship. A sense of unpredictability looms about these people. You know that if they are willing to lie to a ranger, a customer, a client, another business associate, then they are willing to lie to you as well. If they will cheat in one arena of life, there is a good possibility that everything and everybody is up for grabs. So you approach the relationship with caution. You put up walls. Every encounter is guarded. You never know when you might be their next victim.

Think about how you feel when someone shares a bit of juicy gossip with you. On one hand, you feel affirmed that this person has made you a part of the inner circle of people who know the latest scoop. On the other hand, it creates suspicion. If he or she talks about other people in their absence, what's being said about *you* when you're not around?

These are a few of the ways we react to other people's character. At the same time, others are reacting to our character as well. When you put the two forces together, they weave a complex tapestry of relational dynamics. One person's integrity can have a positive influence. Another person may breed animosity. Some of us have been hurt and so devote ourselves to self-protection. Others amble naively through life. As our integrity meshes with the integrity of others in this way, we compound the effect of character on our relationships.

Just look around your neighborhood, your office, your family. It doesn't take a great deal of observation to recognize that God's standard for character was designed for the preservation of relationships. Those who follow it, intentionally or unintentionally, will be rewarded relationally. Those who don't, either out of stubbornness or ignorance, will forfeit the joy of authentic relationships.

Where there is character, there is compatibility.

Where character is lacking, there is conflict.

## A LOOK AT FOUR VITAL RELATIONSHIPS

In your lifetime, you will have some relationships that are lifelong; others, only brief encounters. Some relationships are competitive in nature, while others are inherently edifying. There will be intimate friendships as well as casual acquaintances. But when it comes to examining the effects of character, there are four primary relationships to consider.

### Our Relationship with God

The instant we knowingly compromise our character, a change takes place deep inside us. In that moment we become keenly aware of a disparity between God's standard and the one we are living out. We are filled with a gnawing sense of unworthiness, and we feel distanced from Him. We call this feeling *guilt*.

Once we feel distanced from God, our tendency is to avoid Him. So we move even further away, and the feeling of distance increases. Eventually, we may entertain thoughts that God would never accept us back. This only makes us avoid Him more. Ironically, we begin to treat God with the same avoidance techniques we use on other people. Instead of facing our conflict, we avoid it. We go on with our lives (and often our sin) as if He weren't there.

We may try to rationalize our behavior. We may even go so far as to recreate God in our image. After all, if the real God doesn't accept us the way we are, why not just create a version of God that does? Of course, that doesn't solve anything. It only makes things worse.

To avoid the pursuit of character is to jeopardize one's walk with God. If the development of character is not an intentional pursuit for you, it should come as no surprise that God seems distant and uninterested.

Notice I said "seems." God is *not at all* uninterested. Neither is He distant. But when our purposes and priorities are out of alignment with His, the relationship suffers. God's purpose for your life is to bring your character into conformity with that of His Son—that's what He's doing inside of you. As you begin to focus on that same priority, you will become increasingly aware of His presence and power in your life.

## Relationship with Ourselves

Another important relationship affected by our character is our relationship with ourselves. This is a peculiar thought to some. Normally a relationship requires two parties. But self-image constitutes one of the most important relationships in life. It is a prerequisite for all other human relationships. The way we view ourselves determines how we will interact with God, family, friends, loved ones, and even those we consider to be our enemies.

The absence of character can have a variety of effects on self, depending on the person. When character is compromised, most people experience some form of guilt. In some cases, it's because they've established at least some arbitrary standards of integrity and decency. Guilt is simply a by-product of their failure to meet their own standards. As if they were two people in a single body, one half somehow feels like it has let the other half down. It feels unworthy and unreliable. The result is lowered self-esteem.

God's standards are written on our hearts (see Romans 2:14–16), even if we haven't cobbled together any standards of our own. And when we fail to meet His standards, we feel like failures to some extent.

In addition, we must always deal with the consequences of our character deficit. When we make bad decisions, the fallout can be devastating.

Many of our conflicts are created not by unavoidable factors, but by our own unwise choices. Well aware of our own contribution to our problems, our self-esteem takes another hit. It is difficult to embrace and accept an enemy, and when we act as our own enemy, it makes it more difficult to accept ourselves.

People who are unhappy with themselves always find something to be unhappy about in those around them. Generally speaking, those who are closest to us—our husband, wife, or children—are primary targets. Ironically, it is when we are least happy about the state of our own character that we are quickest to find fault with others. It is human nature to mirror our displeasure with ourselves in our attitudes toward those around us.

In contrast, when our character is hitting on all cylinders, we enjoy a clear conscience. No matter what hardships we may face, we can rest in the knowledge that we have honored God's absolute standard of right and wrong, regardless of what it has cost us. We've done our part. As a result, hardships are not punishment for unwise choices, but are simply the valiant price that must be paid by a person of character. Instead of guilty failures, we feel more like victorious overcomers.

### Our Relationships with Others

This category includes everyone from spouses and family members to business associates and passing strangers. We've already discussed the impact character has on these types of relationships. But what we haven't discussed is the source of almost all interrelational conflict: unmet expectations.

We live in a world where compromise is the ruling principle. You'd think by now that it wouldn't surprise us when someone does us wrong.

Nevertheless, it does. We can accept the general notion that the world is full of evil. But somehow, it never ceases to amaze us that someone would treat *us* unjustly. The audacity! We deserve better.

One reason we respond this way is that we operate from a position of our expectations. If we demonstrate a reasonable measure of character at work, we expect a certain response in return. Likewise, we have expectations for our families, our friends, and even for people we don't know. Some expectations are based on past experience. Others might be based on what we've been told. But as we waltz through life with our delicate system of expectations, we're just begging to have them shattered. We build china shops for a world full of bulls, and we're taken aback when the glass starts breaking.

Everyone carries a personal set of expectations. Unfortunately, as we interact with one another, there's no way we can all emerge unscathed. It's like trying to fit two gunfighters into one little western town—there's just not room enough for both of them. Sooner or later, somebody's bound to get hurt.

At the bottom of all our expectations lies a self-centered motive: We agree to be people of integrity as long as we receive reasonable treatment in return. This small qualification turns the issue of unmet expectations into a character issue. Larry Crabb goes right to the heart of the matter:

> The greatest obstacle to building truly good relationships is justified self-centeredness, a selfishness that, deep in our souls, feels entirely reasonable and therefore acceptable in light of how we've been treated.[4]

Character is not only about *submitting* to God's standard of right and wrong; it also means *surrendering* to God our expectations of others. We aren't willing to suffer the personal cost if it includes being wronged by others, but if we extend anything less than the grace of God to those who wrong us, then we fall short of God's standard. Character involves loving our neighbors as ourselves—even when they don't reciprocate.

Of course, that's a lot easier said than done. But once character becomes a real target, once becoming a man or woman of character becomes your life's ambition, you will see being mistreated by others as an opportunity to demonstrate character, rather than as a setback. Once you relinquish your expectations to God, you will find that you are much less likely to be disappointed by those around you. This being true, you'll find it easier to resist the urge to back away from those who hurt you. Or to retaliate.

If we genuinely trusted God to bring about justice when others treat us wrong, we wouldn't expend our own emotional energy on vengeful thoughts. If we looked to God to meet our needs, we wouldn't be so disappointed when others failed to come through for us. In short, if we had the will to do what was right regardless of personal cost, then we would experience the rewards of character in our relationships. We would learn the age-old lesson that there is much to be gained from every relationship, whether friend or foe.

## Our Community Relationships

The impact of our interaction with others doesn't stop with personal relationships. It has a ripple effect on all the relationships within our community. Eventually, our character is revealed in the dynamics of our homes, our work environment, the church, and every other arena where we're involved.

The collective integrity of a group of people determines the success or failure of that community. In order for our communities to remain functional, the individuals within the community must be functional. Godly character must not only be present, it must be predominant. This is the basic tenet behind the principle of self-government.

The principle of self-government rests on the premise that when a person or entity fails to govern itself internally, it will eventually be governed by outside forces. When a child cannot obey household rules, the parent steps in and implements control. Likewise, when an adult fails to govern himself according to the laws of the land, the appropriate authorities are called in. On a larger scale, when countries fail to govern themselves effectively, they become ripe for revolution, internal coup, or hostile takeover by another country. Regardless of the size or type of the community, the key to its success is the character of its individuals.

The two fronts on which I see this principle played out on a regular basis are the home and the local church. *Character deficiencies are at the heart of every divided home or divided church.* Wherever two or more people are gathered, there will be conflict, tension, and friction. But that, in and of itself, is not the problem. In most cases, those things are healthy. They are normal. After all, the same could be said of your car's engine. But when there is friction and no lubricant, problems develop. When there is no oil, there is eventually a breakdown. When men and women gather as a family or church congregation, there will always be differences; but men and women of character can always find a way to work through their differences without division.

There is always a way to deal with differences in a way that demonstrates respect for all parties. But that assumes adherence to a standard that values respect. It assumes that both parties are committed to doing what's right regardless of the personal cost. Dealing with differences and even conflict successfully requires that all parties place a premium on integrity, honesty, fairness—in other words, character.

Men and women pursuing character know that conflict is simply another opportunity, and they approach it as such. In their minds, there is always a win-win option if both parties put a premium on doing what's right.

## THE COMMITMENT TO CHARACTER

These principles are unfailing because they flow from the nature of our unfailing, unchanging heavenly Father. Man's ability to understand himself is limited to the capacity of his own mind. Our day-to-day problems surpass our problem-solving abilities with overwhelming regularity. And when our efforts fail, we often feel frustrated, confused, or just plain burned out.

Sooner or later, we must come to the conclusion that we are incapable of facing life on our own, relying on our own methods. We simply don't have what it takes. Man can no more be expected to survive the rigors of life on his own than a newborn baby can take on the challenges of life in New York City.

The instructions God has given us are critical to our survival. Without godly virtue, we cause immediate harm to our self-image. Without integrity, it's just a matter of time before we destroy each other. Without character, we inflict untold damage on our communities. The cornerstone of our entire social structure is the condition of the inner person. Just by subscribing to the belief in an absolute standard of right and wrong, we can begin to reverse the subtle encroachment of conflict in our relationships. If we simply commit to do what is right regardless of personal cost, our relationships will prosper.

Ted and Margaret Cook know this to be a fact. On September 17, 1996, this happy couple celebrated their seventy-fifth anniversary. When asked the secret of their marital success, Ted answered, "If you do right, you can get along. I tried to do right all along." When asked if that included flowers and candy on Valentine's Day, Margaret responded, "None of that stuff matters. Being good to me, nice to me, is what I liked."

Margaret isn't the only one who likes that. We all do. Character is about doing what's right. Relationships are about getting along. And in the words of Ted Cook, "If you do right, you can get along." By doing right, we create opportunities for our heavenly Father to advance our relationships from where they are to where He knows they need to be.

# Chapter Four

# THE PROMISE OF CHARACTER

*What lies behind us and what lies before*
*us are tiny matters compared to what lies within us.*
RALPH WALDO EMERSON

At the edge of a rocky overlook in the Appalachian foothills stands a lone, two-hundred-year-old evergreen tree. At first glance, the scene looks like a snapshot taken during a violent storm. Bent by two centuries of strong winds blowing up the steep ridge, the thick, gnarled trunk leans hard to one side. Its heavy branches stretch longingly toward the mountain's peak.

Botanists call this phenomenon the Krummholz Effect. Constant winds from one direction have left the tree frozen in this distressed posture. Like an oversize Japanese bonsai tree, it appears half-dead as it clings to the ridge. Only the soft, golden glow of the afternoon sun and the playful twitching of its delicate needles reveal that the old tree is thriving peacefully.

Through the years, it has defied heavy snows, hailstorms, and the steady westerly winds rising off the valley floor. From its vulnerable view of the endless ridges and valleys, it has seen conditions that would snap most trees right in half. Nevertheless, it stands alone at the edge of a vast landscape.

On the outside, it looks worn and ready to topple. But a look inside tells the real story. Its roots reach deep into the rich mountain soil, producing a steady supply of nourishing sap. The boughs, though severely bent, are positioned to absorb the brunt of nature's blows without incident. And each year, the old tree yields lush green needles and an abundance of fertile cones.

What's the secret? How can anything face such relentless opposition and survive? The answer lies below the surface. For two centuries, the elements have hurled their assaults against the old tree. But while storms raged on the outside, the tree was quietly developing an inner support system to sustain it. Every gust of wind sent the roots clawing deeper into the soil, expanding their tenacious grip on the mountain. Year after year, the weight of ice and snow caused the strained boughs to grow thicker and stronger. On the outside, it may be an oddity. But inside, it's a picture of health.

We are all, like trees, subjected to the stormy elements of life. And when the storms come, we either snap or grow stronger. What makes the difference is not the ferocity of the storm but the depth of our character. The outcome depends on the condition of our inner person. Like the old tree, we need a system capable of sustaining and nurturing us through the relentless cycles of life.

Godly character is a system that sustains and nurtures our inner man. It enables us not only to survive the storms of life, but to thrive. We could go on forever talking about the tangible, observable benefits of character, but in addition to these external advantages, character also adds immeasurable value to our lives in two internal ways: *spiritual intimacy* and *emotional stamina.*

While both of these benefits are referenced throughout Scripture, perhaps they are best summarized in Psalm 15. In five short verses, this psalm describes a person of character:

> O LORD, who may abide in Your tent?
>> Who may dwell on Your holy hill?
> He who walks with integrity, and works righteousness,
>> And speaks truth in his heart.
> He does not slander with his tongue,
>> Nor does evil to his neighbor,
> Nor takes up a reproach against his friend;
>> In whose eyes a reprobate is despised,
> But who honors those who fear the LORD;
>> He swears to his own hurt and does not change;
> He does not put out his money at interest,
>> Nor does he take a bribe against the innocent.
> He who does these things will never be shaken.

## SPIRITUAL INTIMACY: THE INSIDE TRACK WITH GOD

A correlation exists between our personal righteousness, or our character, and our ability to know God intimately. The psalmist promises that the person who pursues character gains the privilege of experiencing a special relationship with the Father. Psalm 15 describes the difference between those who know God from a distance and those who know Him intimately.

You might not think of yourself as a person who longs to know God. Using the term *intimacy* to describe someone's relationship to God may even seem strange to you, conjuring images of all-day prayers or living in a catatonic state of deep spiritual meditation.

But chances are, there is something in you that longs at times for the privilege of intimacy with your heavenly Father. If you have ever faced a crisis and wanted to ask, "Why, Lord?" then you've longed for it. If you've ever prayed for peace and perspective during a time of uncertainty, you've wanted it. If you have ever been afraid or lonely and just needed comfort, you've wanted the benefits that come from knowing God better. We have all had times in our lives when just a word—an insight, an assurance that He was there—would make all the difference in the world. There is a part of you that longs for intimacy with God. You want an inside track.

This desire is most pronounced when we face those inevitable, unanswerable, perplexing questions that are a part of all our lives. And the longing to know paves the way to knowing Him. Seeking answers to our deepest and frequently unspoken questions is often the catalyst for seeking Him.

The psalmist asks, "Who may dwell in your sanctuary? Who may live on your holy hill?" (NIV). The questions assume that these two things are worth seeking.

Neither, however, sound very appealing.

Who wants to live in a church building or a monastery on a lonely mountain?

The people of the psalmist's culture knew that the term *sanctuary* referred to the tabernacle, or tent, where God resided. The "holy hill" was the hill in Jerusalem, where the permanent temple was eventually built. To have access to these places was to have access to God.

The Israelites of the day thought of God as dwelling in the Ark of the

Covenant inside the tabernacle. In their way of thinking, wherever the Ark was, that's where God was. The closer you were to the Ark and the tent, the closer you were to God. The further you were from the Ark, the further you were from God. They believed this so deeply that they took the Ark of the Covenant with them into battle. And who could blame them?

So when you take the psalmist's queries, steeped in ancient Jewish culture, and translate them into our language, this passage asks and answers one of the most relevant questions imaginable: *Who gets an inside track with God?* The implication here is that intimacy with God is a real possibility.

Psalm 15 makes it clear that this privilege is reserved for men and women of character. Look again at the description:

- Their walk is blameless.
- They do what is right.
- They tell the truth.
- They don't gossip.
- They don't mistreat people.
- They side with those who are right.
- They keep their word.
- They lend money to those in need without interest.
- They don't take advantage of people for financial gain.

Clearly, character paves the way to intimacy with God.

Initially, this idea may sound somewhat pretentious. Even unchristian. But that isn't the case at all. Throughout Scripture, God is described as having a personality. Over and over we see Him relating to mankind in much the same way we relate to one another. In fact, the rules that govern human relationships are very similar to the rules that govern our relationship with the Father.

Three elements are always present in a healthy relationship:

1. Respect
2. Trust
3. Communication

A quality relationship with someone—anyone—requires all three of these elements. The same is true of your relationship with God. When we acknowledge that God's standard is *the* standard, we demonstrate respect. When we commit to follow God's standard regardless of what it costs us, we trust Him. As we seek to understand His standard more thoroughly, and as we run up against our inability to live out His standard consistently, we communicate with Him.

The pursuit of character inevitably becomes the pursuit of God.

### Putting the Shoe on the Other Foot

Turn it around for a minute. You've probably known someone in your past who pursued a relationship with you for all the wrong reasons. Once you got close to that person, you realized he or she had a hidden agenda. Do you remember how that felt?

How do you respond, internally, to a person like that? Do you open up and become more transparent? Of course not. You become cautious. You suspect actions and motives. You rehearse old conversations and think, *So that's why he said that.*

Think a minute. If your interaction with God is focused primarily on getting something from Him, what does that say about your relationship? You aren't coming to Him on terms that warrant a relationship of intimacy.

Still, God listens to our self-centered prayers. Sometimes He actually grants our requests. But as long as we see Him only as a means to our ends, we will never experience intimacy. We will never truly know Him. For this unique depth of relationship is reserved for those who respect Him, trust Him, and are willing to communicate honestly with Him. It is withheld from those who dishonor Him by treating Him like a mere vending machine.

There's a correlation between your personal holiness and your intimacy with God. There's a direct relationship between your willingness to obey God and His willingness to reveal Himself to you. This is *the* primary benefit of character. Character brings a heightened sense of intimacy with God—an intimacy available only through the pursuit of Christlike character.

## His Closest Friends

During His ministry on earth, Jesus modeled this cause-and-effect relationship. He reserved a level of intimacy for a select group—the ones who had left everything to follow Him. They respected Him. They trusted Him. And they were in constant communication. No, the twelve apostles weren't perfect. But they had left their businesses, their families, and their reputations to pursue a relationship with Him. He was their priority.

Further evidence of this is found in an incident that took place immediately following the telling of a parable. The meaning of these stories was not always clear, and apparently this began to bother the disciples. On this occasion the disciples pulled Jesus aside and asked Him why He wasn't more direct with His audience. He said, "Because it has been given to you to know the mysteries of the kingdom of heaven, but to them it has not been given" (Matthew 13:11, NKJV).

Jesus was suggesting to His disciples that there would always be people who remained out on the fringe, relationally. There would always be curious onlookers who had a distant interest in Jesus. But there were special insights reserved only for those in His inner circle. Did Jesus love the multitudes? Yes. He died for them as well as the twelve. But the multitudes did not know Jesus like the twelve. He chose to reveal Himself to them at a deeper level.

Later, Jesus took them aside and explained the meaning of each parable. To His special friends, it had been "given…to know the mysteries of the kingdom of heaven." Their unique calling and sacrifice enabled them to enjoy a deeper level of intimacy with the Savior than was enjoyed by the masses.

God sent a similar message to the people of Israel through the prophet Jeremiah: "You will seek me and find me when you seek me with all your heart" (Jeremiah 29:13, NIV).

One summer, in the late afternoon, I was walking down the beach by myself. The tide was out, giving the sensation that the beach went on forever. The only sounds I could hear were the occasional call of the gulls and the distant laughter of children playing. As I walked along, the air was noticeably still. I remember thinking how odd it was that there wasn't even a breeze. After walking for about a mile, I turned around to head back to the hotel.

And when I did, something strange happened.

Suddenly, from out of nowhere, there was a breeze. I didn't feel it as much as I heard it whistling in my ears. Where had it come from? It had been there all along—I just wasn't aware of it. As long as it was at my back, I didn't hear or feel it. But as soon as I faced the other way, my ears immediately sensed its presence.

The same is true of God. As long as we have our backs turned to Him—pursuing our own interests and desires, living life the way we think it should be lived—we are less aware of His presence. He's there, but we remain unaware. Once we begin prioritizing our lives around His values and principles, it's as if He comes alive to us. There's a heightened sense of the reality of God. But again, the sense of His presence is reserved for those who have turned in His direction.

## EMOTIONAL STAMINA: DELIVERED THROUGH THE STORMS

The second internal benefit of being a man or woman of character is found at the end of Psalm 15. After describing the person of character in detail, the psalmist concludes, "He who does these things will never be shaken."

Now this is a benefit you don't experience immediately. It's one of those things that comes from weeks, months, or even years of investing in one's character. It's the result of adopting a lifestyle. The image the psalmist paints is that of two trees in a storm. While the same storm sweeps over both trees with the same force, one tree is destroyed while the other is left standing.

So it is with men and women of character. They are not delivered from the storms of life, but they are delivered *through* them. Their roots go deep. Their faith is strong. Their resolve is unwavering.

Their pursuit of Christlikeness gains for them the unique privilege of saying to God, "God, I'm just doing what You told me to do. You got me into this. It's up to You to get me through it." They deliberately and sincerely cast their deepest and most intimate cares upon God, and they live with confidence that He is going to care for them (see 1 Peter 5:7).

There is no place in the world more secure than the middle of God's will. In fact, it's the only real security there is. To pursue a life of character, then, is to prepare for the storms of life. Remember, "He who does these things will never be shaken."

What's the reason men and women of character will never be shaken? What's their secret? Just this: They understand that navigating the storms of life is not their responsibility.

Maybe things are going great for you now. Or maybe you're picking up the pieces from a recent squall. It could be that you don't see any real reason to commit to this process right away. But count on it, there are storms on the horizon. Life is just that way. And the best preparation you could make is to begin developing intimacy with God.

Ironically, the greatest tragedy of missing this process isn't that your marriage might fall apart. Or that you'll flounder in your career. Or that you'll be lonely the rest of your life. As tragic as those things are, the greatest tragedy of refusing to pursue the character of Christ is that *you'll miss God.*

He'll be right there at your back, but you'll miss Him.

Yes, there is a price to be paid for becoming a person of character. But it's not nearly as high as the price of pursuing the ways of this fallen world. For to neglect your character is to forfeit the assurance of God's presence in the storms of life.

Character paves the way to intimacy with God. To know Him is to trust Him. To trust Him is to live with the confidence that He will not allow you to be shaken. That's the ultimate promise of character. It is the promise of His presence. A presence you cannot possibly miss.

# Chapter Five

# AN INSIDE JOB

*May the inner man and the outer be one.*
SOCRATES

A canopy of heavy clouds hung just above the airport. Somewhere overhead in the hovering mist, a fully loaded 757 banked to the right and began its final approach to runway 24R. The pilots could see nothing. The captain anxiously scanned the instrument panels as the aircraft gradually gave up valuable altitude. His moist palms clenched the yoke as he guided the plane along the prescribed course. Their sole source of guidance was an airport beacon that emitted a steady radio signal to indicate their position. Without it, they were lost.

The young copilot eyed the altimeter, monitoring their descent. One thousand feet...nine hundred...eight hundred.... Repeatedly he scanned the gauges, checking air speed, rate of descent, glide path, and glide slope. Then he began the process over again. He longed to glance out the window, looking for a break in the clouds and the ground below. But his job required him to focus on the repetitive task of scanning instrument readouts and checking tolerances.

The flight had been long. They had encountered strong, steady head-winds along the way. And after more than an hour of circling the airport, they had burned a lot of fuel. Relentless turbulence had rocked the craft for half a day, and the monotony was beginning to wear on the crew's nerves. Heavy rains roared against the nose of the plane. The windshield wipers cranked out their monotonous rhythm: *whomp, whomp, whomp, whomp.* The cockpit felt like a broom closet, and as the intensity grew, the room was getting smaller by the minute.

Though he could see nothing, the captain bore all the confidence of an eagle gliding purposefully toward its target. "Auto go, auto land," he methodically announced to the crew as he scanned the flight data. The air-craft's tracking devices were locked in on the signal of the beacon. Now it was a matter of trust.

Once again, the copilot cross-checked the instruments, watching for any deviations from the norm. As the ground quickly came up to meet them, he had to be ready to initiate a "go-around" immediately. The ver-tical airspeed indicator confirmed their rate of descent. They were on the correct glide slope.

Everything looked good, but in the tension of the moment, it didn't *feel* right. The copilot's instincts told him they were headed for an aborted approach. The forecast was dismal, and he reasoned they wouldn't get the visibility they needed to land. But despite what he was feeling, he kept silent and continued the landing procedures.

In a moment, the captain would have to make a decision. Within a window of only one or two seconds, he would either declare visual contact and take over the landing, or abort and begin the process of reversing the heavy plane's downward momentum.

Four hundred feet...three hundred. Still, the dense clouds prevailed. With his left hand resting on the throttle, the copilot rotated his palm toward the back of the handle until he felt the two buttons that, if pushed, would terminate the approach and initiate an automatic ascent. His index finger quivered slightly as he held it in the ready position. Two hundred feet...one hundred...

Suddenly, a loud thump shook the plane as it slammed through a pocket of turbulence. The copilot swallowed the lump in his throat. Then, like a whale plunging into the quiet safety of the ocean's depths, the giant aircraft dropped below the ceiling of clouds and into the clear. The air was peaceful and calm. Instantly, they could see for miles. And runway 24R, situated precisely in the path of their approach, seemed to sprawl out for miles awaiting their arrival.

"I've got it," announced the captain.

The copilot sighed a deep sigh.

## CLOUDY VISION

There are times when all of us find it difficult to navigate through the turbulence of life. Circumstances close in around us, narrowing our perspective. We lose our passion for living. Terms like *purpose* and *destiny* elicit no emotion. Our goals no longer seem worth striving for. Our surroundings distract us. And God seems a million miles away.

But in the middle of those dark times there is a beacon beckoning for our attention. There is a signal worth locking in on.

It is the beacon of integrity.

It is God's still, small voice calling us to become men and women of character. It is a constant signal emitted from the Spirit within us to remind us of what matters most—matters of the heart, right and wrong, love.

But like the pilot in the storm, it is our nature to look out at the world around us and want to reach for the controls. We feel compelled to take over, to alter our course. Our common sense tells us that pursuing character is great for the blue-sky days, but storms are a different matter. Storms are an exception. When life becomes turbulent, it's every man for himself. In times of crisis, we decide that pursuing character may not be in our best interest.

But nothing could be further from the truth. For nothing tests, shapes, and strengthens our character like periods of turbulence. And yet it is in these difficult times that so many of us look elsewhere for direction. When the clouds of circumstance close in around us, we tend to lock in on something other than the absolutes God has given as a beacon to guide us home safely. And consequently, we find ourselves somewhere we never intended to go.

Just about every week I talk to people who say things like…

"I don't think God loves me."

"I don't think God really cares about me."

"God doesn't answer my prayers."

When I ask why, they tell me about the circumstances of their lives. They tell me stories of sickness, death, divorce, prodigal children, financial ruin.

As all of us are prone to do from time to time, these hurting folks are looking for God in all the wrong places. They are evaluating His presence and concern by how well He meets their expectations. They are taking their own personal agenda and measuring God's faithfulness by how well He meets it.

This works fine until God takes them someplace they never expected. The minute adversity arises, it seems like there's a glitch in the system, when in reality, everything is still right on track. The problem is not their circumstances, but how they interpret them.

While we're frantically looking for God on the outside, He can always be found on the inside. That's where He's hard at work. That's where He does His *best* work.

Sure, God is intimately concerned about our circumstances. He doesn't miss a single detail, and He promises to meet a believer's every need. But we tend to place much more importance on the outer things than God ever intended. His main focus is not so much on the seen, but the unseen. For this reason, if we're going to gain a greater appreciation and understanding of what God is up to in our lives, we're going to have to give some quality attention to what He is up to *inside* of us.

## A CHANGE OF VIEW

We give our best time to the external world. Most of our energy is focused on trying to control our circumstances. We don't want it too hot or too cold, too poor or too rich, too old-fashioned or too trendy, too old or too new. Whether it's politically correct, socially correct, or religiously correct, each of us makes a pretty good stab at being "correct."

Unfortunately, this leaves us little or no time to focus on our inner person. And the tragedy is, as long as we allow the outside world to dictate our activities, we will miss out on what God is up to.

When a student pilot practices for an instrument rating, the instructor often places a veil over the airplane windows to teach him or her to focus on the instruments. We could all take a lesson from that example. Once in a while, all Christians should put up a veil, so to speak, and practice focusing on what's happening on the inside.

All of us are susceptible to putting our focus in the wrong place. But as long as your priority in life is anything other than the character of Jesus Christ, you will always be prone to look for God in your circumstances. When you do, you will miss Him, misunderstand Him, and doubt Him. And it won't be His fault. Because all the time you feel that way, He's very much there and very much at work. He is committed to His original plan and agenda for your life. And that is, to work inside of you and transform you from the inside out.

Until you embrace this paradigm of the spiritual life, you will have a difficult time turning your focus away from what's happening around you. You will continue trying to measure and evaluate God's love and involvement in your life by your circumstances. And you will overlook His most significant activity: the activity taking place inside you.

Often, when Christians can't make sense of what God is doing in their lives, they begin to compartmentalize. There is the *religious* side of life, and there is the *secular* side of life. The religious side includes all situations in which God is perceived to be interested or directly involved. These include church activities, acts of service, and benevolences performed in the name of God.

All other activities are then lumped into the secular category. These include work, recreation, friendships, and family, to name just a few. *Secular* then becomes a catchall—a place where we put the parts of our lives that we determine are not of interest to God. As far as we're concerned, He doesn't want access to them, nor do we concern ourselves with presenting them to Him.

People who compartmentalize allocate a certain portion of their lives to God but maintain control of the rest. They do their part when it comes to religious duties, like attending church, but fail to take an active role in conforming their whole lives to the image of Christ.

But our heavenly Father is interested in every aspect of our lives. He wants to transform us from the inside out to reflect the character of His Son. But when we consciously or unconsciously compartmentalize, we lock God out of vital portions of our lives. As a result, we can *never* make sense of the circumstances of life. God seems a distant, uncaring creator of a universe governed by luck and random chance.

In most cases, people who compartmentalize do so by default. Since they can't see evidence of God in their circumstances, they assume He's not there. Why? Because they're looking in the wrong place.

Let's face it, it's a lot easier to focus on your career, your family, and your friends. At least you can see how all that works! You can see when you're making progress or when some detail needs special attention. But real life begins on the inside. And every day, if you're a believer, God is there pushing, pulling, working, to create something wonderful from the inside out.

## GOD THE CONSUMMATE INVESTOR

The world is full of hurting people. People who have been injured by family members, ripped off by total strangers, and neglected by the system. With so many legitimate needs around us, it's easy to wonder why God doesn't do more to fix our problems. But what our human eyes so often fail to see is that while we struggle with the woes of this world, God's main occupation is preparing us for the world to come. The focus of what God is doing in your life takes place *in* you, not *around* you. And for good reason.

God is a good investor. He's not going to waste His investment in a body or a world that is destined to pass away. His money is on the part that's going to last forever—the soul, the spirit, the inside person. We Christians, however, get that turned around. We spend our time, energy, and resources on the outer person. And we miss God. That's why there are times in our lives when it seems like He's so far away. Think about it. Most of our prayers have to do with our health, our wealth, and our social life. And when we experience a setback or grow impatient, we say, "God, where are You?"

At the same time, we fail to pray for the things that will benefit us for eternity. If God answered all of our prayers, our character would suffer. For in most cases, our prayers center around the removal of the very circumstances He is using to conform us to His image.

Every day, eager investors scope out the trading floor on Wall Street looking for tips. In addition to doing his own research, a thorough analyst knows there are certain key people to watch to help determine whether a stock's value will rise or fall. Sometimes the least little flinch can cause a flurry of trading. If it looks like somebody knows something, it catches people's attention.

In your life and in mine, the consummate Trader has spoken. God has purchased a million shares of your inner person. That should tell us something. The question we should be asking is not "Why doesn't God do something?" but "What is God up to, and how can I get in on it?" If God's primary concern is our character, that should give us a pretty good idea about where to place our focus.

After all, God isn't just going on a hunch. He's got insider information.

## GOD THE DILIGENT WORKER

In the pages that follow, we're going to look at several things you can do to work alongside God to develop your character. But first you must understand what He's been up to since the day you were born. Once you see what God has planned for your character—and why—you'll be more motivated and better equipped to get in on it.

Nowhere is this better summarized than in Philippians 2:12–13:

> Continue to work out your salvation with fear and trembling, for it is God who works in you to will and to act according to his good purpose.
>
> N I V

In this passage the apostle Paul stresses a couple of things for us to note. First, he tells his readers that God is working inside of them. It doesn't get much plainer than that! Second, he tells them that this work is going on *right now.* The verb is in the present tense. It's happening now. It was happening when Paul wrote it, and it was still going on when his readers finally received the letter.

Some guy from Philippi might have written back, "Hey Paul, you don't even know me. How do you know what God's up to in my life?"

The fact is, God is at work in all believers. That means you. It's present tense; it's constant. When you're tempted, when you give in to temptation, or when you tempt someone else, God is still at work. While you're busy at work, juggling your children, or dreaming about your boyfriend or girlfriend, He's still at work. He has purchased His investment at a price, and He's making certain that it goes up in value. He won't quit or give up. And someday He will complete His work, and we will be presented before His throne as holy, blameless, and perfect.

I remember the first time I really thought about Philippians 2:12–13. I said to myself, *I'm certainly not aware of anything going on.* Most of the time we don't feel any different. We go through spiritual and emotional dry times, and somebody says, "Hey, what's God doing in your life?" "Well…nothing," we mumble. Most of the time it seems like He's not up to much. It could be that you are so unfamiliar with His ways you simply can't see what He's up to. When you're not familiar with His ways, it is difficult to recognize His hand at work.

I know a woman named Helen who worked for years in the abortion industry. Before she came to Christ she didn't give much thought to the fetal tissue the clinic discarded every day. To her it was just tissue. But then she became a believer. The couple that led her to Christ told her to read 2 Corinthians 5:17. They assured her that once she became a Christian she would become a new creature in Christ. She took the words literally—she thought she would look different. After praying the sinner's prayer, Helen looked in the mirror—but there stood the same Helen. She was disappointed and wondered if her prayer had "taken."

It wasn't until the next morning, when she showed up for work, that she became aware of the change that had taken place. For years she had seen only tissue as she witnessed the abortions at her clinic. But on this particular morning she saw dead babies. Something *had* changed inside of Helen. And the change in her inner person resulted in several lifestyle changes to her outer person.

That is God's way. Every minute of every day He's on the job in our lives.

## CHRIST THE PERFECT MODEL

The next thing you need to know about God's work in you is that it's designed with God's purposes in mind. Remember all those disillusioned people who pass through my office, trying to measure God's involvement in their lives by looking at their circumstances? Here's your chance to avoid that trap.

The end result of God's work is not measured by how smoothly our lives run, or by how rich or how beautiful we become. It's based on a very specific agenda that God set a long time ago. His goal is to recreate in you and me the character of Jesus Christ. Paul said it this way: "For those God foreknew he also predestined to be conformed to the likeness of his Son" (Romans 8:29, NIV).

That's what God has been working to accomplish in you, to make you more like His own Son. This doesn't mean He wants you to start wearing a robe and sandals, grow a beard, and add "Verily, verily" to the beginning of every sentence. His goal isn't to make you smarter or to alter your personality. After all, He's a God of variety; He's never made any two things exactly alike.

What it means is that when you became a Christian, there was placed in you a brand-new potential for character. The life of Christ was planted in you, and your potential for good, for character, went up about a thousand percent. In fact, it's now equal to that of Jesus Christ. That doesn't mean you're going to be God. (I know that comes as a shock.) But it does mean that you have been given the life of Christ along with all its potential. And now that you have this potential *in* you, what God wants to do is fan the flame.

Sometimes it gets hot.

It's not always very comfortable.

But on that day when you and I have the finish line in view, ready to cross that tape and complete our race, we'll understand that our character was infinitely more important than our comfort.

# Chapter Six

# THE HARD WAY

*A man's success lies not in what cards he is dealt,*
*but in whether he bothers to pick them up and play them.*
BEN ORTLIP

There exists an all-too-common heart condition that, if left unchecked, will impede character development. This condition is so serious that it will thwart your every attempt to advance your character in a positive direction. The Scriptures refer to this malady as a *hard heart.*

Perhaps the best definition I've heard of what it means to have a hard heart came from one of my graduate school professors. He defined a hard heart as "overexposure and under-response to truth." When we are repeatedly exposed to a particular truth and yet refuse to embrace and apply it, we are actively developing a hardened heart. When we say no to God repeatedly in a particular area of life, we are developing a hard heart. When we hear the truth, and hear the truth, and hear the truth—and keep ignoring it, ignoring it, ignoring it—our hearts grow hard.

A similar thing happens to your hands when you work in the yard or lift weights without gloves. At first the rake or the barbell rubs against the skin, and it hurts. There is a sensitivity to the consequences created by the friction. But after a while, the skin begins to toughen up.

Gradually, you develop calluses.

Eventually, you feel nothing at all.

Your skin gets so thick that it insulates your nerve endings, and you just can't feel it anymore. The sensitivity is gone.

That's what happens to our hearts. When we repeatedly say no to God, our hearts can become so hard that we no longer even *detect* His voice. He's still speaking, but we can't hear. He's still at work, but we are in no position to respond. We've lost our spiritual sensitivity.

The real tragedy of a hard heart is its long-range consequences. When we continually shut Him out of one area of our lives, it affects our ability to discern His voice in other areas as well. And once an individual loses the ability to discern the promptings of God's Spirit, he or she becomes open to just about anything.

Whenever God's standard conflicts with our personality, our lifestyle, or our circumstances, an interesting phenomenon takes place. Our first instinct is to tweak His standard; we adjust it just a little bit to fit our lifestyle. It's nothing personal. It's simply human nature. We have a natural propensity to change the rules on God. We tend to change His commands to fit our personality, our present lifestyle, or our current circumstances. I've never met anyone who didn't struggle with this.

In fact, as Christians, we are masters at this game. We've had years of practice, hearing the truth and dodging the bullets. We've long since perfected our moves. And so, subconsciously, we emphasize those parts of Scripture that fit our personalities and standing in life. And when confronted with truths that conflict with our personalized version of Christianity, we downplay them.

Without thinking about it, we assign a value to various issues based on how they fit our lifestyle and goals. Sure, we know what God has said about those "other things." But we convince ourselves that those other things are not all that important to God.

## "THAT MAY BE TRUE, BUT..."

You've probably experienced this yourself. Every once in a while, you'll hear a sermon that hits so close to home, it hurts a little bit. And instantly, you start looking for a way to ease out of it. You think, *Well, yeah, that's true, but I have all these other issues to deal with, too.* Or, *I know that's what the Bible says, but it will have to wait because I'm just not ready for that.* Or, *My situation is different. My circumstances are unusual. My past has made me the way I am.* And all the while, you can't wait to get out to the car so you can turn on the radio, tune in the ballgame, and forget about what you've just heard.

There's just one problem. When we change God's standard, it isn't God's standard anymore. Unknowingly, we create a caricature of Christianity—one that doesn't accurately reflect what God truly thinks. Instead, it exaggerates certain features, distorts some, and minimizes others.

Most of us are so good at this technique that we practice it without even realizing it. And ironically, the more we do it, the better we feel about ourselves. Let's imagine the following scenario.

The responsibility-minded dad marches up the stairs and bangs on the door of his teenager's bedroom. He opens the door and turns off the CD player and lectures for thirty minutes about his son's music. The teenager can't make out all the words, but it comes across something like this:

"You're not going to listen to this music anymore. It's going to tear up your mind and your soul. It's of the devil and blah, blah, blah, blah, blah. And we're going to leave you up here to think about it while we go downstairs and turn on the television and watch the visual equivalent of what you've been listening to. But, of course, that's different because...because it just is. Blah, blah, blah, blah, if you know what's good for you."

It's easy to see what's going on in this family. We've all done something similar. Basically, the parents in this picture just don't like the music. And let's face it, it's easy to find something wrong with music that you don't particularly like. But when the crusade is over, these same parents will sit down and entertain themselves visually with the very things they're so against letting their child listen to.

And we tell ourselves, *Well, that's different. That's just how I unwind at the end of the day. I'm an adult; I can handle that. Besides, there was just that one part, and they really didn't show anything...*

In another household there lives a very disciplined lady. She loves doing Bible studies, leading Sunday school classes, having long quiet times, and memorizing verses. She wouldn't think of missing church. She's there for the early service, the late service, candlelight service, communion service, and prayer service. When it comes to the accepted spiritual disciplines, she is faultless.

But at the same time, this same woman is disrespectful to her husband. She refuses to submit to his leadership. She quotes Scripture at him. She seeks to intimidate him with her "spirituality."

So what's wrong with this picture? Like the rest of us, she has simply focused in on the things that come naturally. She doesn't keep the whole counsel of God. She's de-emphasized the things that don't come easily, and so she feels good about herself.

We all struggle with this. Consequently, most of us live with a distorted picture of Christianity. We remold the Christian life to fit our own life. And when we do, we become guilty of a sin we don't hear much about anymore: *idolatry.*

One of the most confusing and yet fascinating stories I heard growing up was the story of Moses' going up on Mount Sinai to receive the Law. I can still remember the pictures in the storybook—the clouds surrounding the mountain, and the people gathered around a big golden calf. Moses disappeared up Mount Sinai, and the people said to themselves, "Okay, Moses is dead. We need something to worship." So they gathered their gold and made a big calf. Then they bowed down and began to worship it.

Even as a kid, I used to think, *How stupid is that? To create something yourself, and then worship it. I mean, you* made *it!* For years I just thought that was the craziest idea. Idolatry didn't appear to be something I would wrestle with as a twenty-first-century Christian.

But I was wrong.

## HEART CHECK

As we allow our hearts to harden toward God, we edit His program. We de-emphasize and reemphasize to the point where we end up worshiping a god who doesn't exist. We create him ourselves. He may bear a striking resemblance to the God of the Bible, but our god is personalized. Custommade. A variation on the real thing.

It is an idol.

Here's the bottom line. You can worship the God of purity and holiness. Or you can worship a god that simply makes you feel accomplished, affirms all your strengths, and never touches your tender spots. But they aren't the same god. God is committed to reshaping your inner person. He moved in to strengthen your weaknesses, not simply to celebrate your strengths.

We all struggle with sin. We all fall to temptation from time to time. All of us have character flaws we aren't even aware of. A hard heart is not a heart that is necessarily in conscious rebellion against God. It is a heart that no longer feels the *conviction* of God. It is a heart that has grown insensitive to the voice of God.

So how do you determine if you have a hard heart? It isn't always obvious. After all, hardness translates into numbness, and numbness, by definition, is sometimes difficult to detect. It is possible to maintain an impeccable, religious routine while our hearts are as hard as steel. In fact, it is human nature to try to compensate for our disobedience by over-achieving in other areas. As a result, a surprising number of the world's hard-hearted people are tremendously religious people.

So how do we evaluate our situation? How do we know if we have grown numb and calloused to the promptings of the Holy Spirit in our lives?

The true test of hard-heartedness is found in a simple equation: The degree of one's hard-heartedness is equal to the disparity between what grieves that person and what grieves God.

The questions to ask are, Am I grieved by the same things that grieve God? Do I feel what God feels? Am I bothered by the things that bother God? Is my heart in sync with His?

Every week through the media of movies, videos, and television, Christians entertain themselves with depictions of the very sins for which Christ died. Yet in most cases, these Christians are not the least bit grieved by this. For some reason, it doesn't strike us as sinful, especially if we are "of age." After all, the movie rating system says we are old enough to handle these things. So what's the problem? Consequently, scenes that would break the heart of God elicit laughter and cheers from His children. And worst of all, we rarely give it a second thought.

Perhaps you've never given much thought to how God feels about the things you call entertainment. After all, you were just unwinding, relaxing with some friends. But the reason it didn't bother you is that you aren't sensitive to it. And that is the nature of a hard heart. *When what grieves God no longer grieves you, your heart is hard. When what bothers God doesn't bother you anymore, your heart is hard.*

Your response to entertainment is just one way to evaluate the status of your heart. There are many others. For example, pick up your Bible and read. What grieved the heart of God in the Old Testament? What grieved the heart of Jesus in the New Testament? How do those same things strike you? Do they elicit any emotion? If so, you are probably sensitive to God's heart. You may not be perfectly obedient in those areas, but at least your heart is pliable. However, if something grieves God in Scripture, but it leaves you wondering if He might have overreacted a little, you may have some work to do.

You could be growing numb.

## TAKING NOTES

If someone spent a week carefully watching your lifestyle—what you laugh at, where you go, what you allow into your mind—what conclusions would he draw about your God? How would the picture he developed compare to the picture of God we find in Scripture? What if he concluded that the things that seem so important to you must also be important to the God you worship? What if he assumed that your priorities reflect His priorities? What if he took his cue about what grieves your God by watching what grieves you? Would there be many similarities between the God of the Bible and the god you follow? Or would there be such a huge discrepancy that this observer would get an entirely wrongheaded idea of the God of Christianity?

Sure, I know nobody's perfect. But I'm not talking about where we *are*. I'm talking about where we are *headed*. The tragedy of a hard heart is that it distorts our sense of direction. We lose our bearings. A hard heart blinds our eyes to the beacon of Christ's character—the reminder of His ultimate intention for our lives. In that way, a hard heart short-circuits our pursuit of character.

Character is acknowledging that life isn't about doing what's good for *me*, or what's easy for *me*, or what comes naturally to *me*. Character is about being conformed to His image, not conforming Him to ours. If we claim to be God-followers, and yet our lifestyle reflects values and standards different from God's, we need to rethink which deity we are really following.

God or a god.

## SOFTENING OUR HEARTS

After years of working with teenagers, nurturing my marriage, and guiding the development of my children, I've learned an important principle: The more I love someone, the less I am able to tolerate the things that hurt him or her.

In the same way, the more concern I have for a group of people, the more concerned I am about the things that grieve them. As my love increases, my tolerance of the things that bring pain to my loved ones decreases.

Before I started working with teenagers, I was somewhat neutral about several issues they faced. But once I got involved with students and they became a part of my life, once I saw a few lives ripped apart through involvement with some of these things I had never really felt strongly about, all of that changed. I developed a passionate disdain for the things that hurt them.

When you love someone, you become sensitive to and intolerant of the things that could cause them potential harm. The same is true about your love for God. Your love for Christ will be reflected in what you tolerate in your life. Facing the reality of a hard heart usually represents a turning point. It is a question of lordship—it boils down to whose rules you're going to play by. Jesus said it this way: "If you love Me, you will keep My commandments" (John 14:15).

Overcoming a hard heart is not about drumming up some sort of pseudo-guilt over things you really don't feel guilty about. Our hearts are transformed through fellowship with the Savior. Only He can make your heart tender and sensitive again. Pursue that relationship, and your heart problems will clear up over time.

Remember how you felt when you became a Christian? Remember how willing you were to do whatever God asked? There was a high level of trust and certainty. You felt God could be trusted, so you stepped out in faith and looked expectantly for Him to intervene. God hasn't changed. He can still be trusted. He still has your best interests in mind.

If you sense that you are suffering from a hard heart, there's only one way to move forward: You've got to go back. You must return to that time when your heart was pliable and sensitive to His Spirit.

Character requires a sensitive heart. To develop character amidst the numbing climate of our society, you cannot afford to develop calluses. You cannot risk operating with blind spots. Before you read any further, search your heart. Is anything there off-limits to the Lord? Are you keeping any area excluded from His lordship? When God exposes your darkness to the light of His truth, how do you respond?

# Chapter Seven

# A PROCESS CALLED
# RENEWAL

*Character is what you are in the dark.*
DWIGHT L. MOODY

The weather was calm over Huffman Prairie on the morning of June 23, 1905. After completing a lengthy checklist, Orville Wright climbed to the controls of the Wright Flyer III. It had been nearly two years since the highly publicized flight at Kitty Hawk had captured the world's imagination. Two years since the flood of telegrams requesting exclusive rights to the Wright brothers' story. The race for manned flight had been won, and now aviation scientists from all over the world were abandoning their exotic prototypes and scrambling to learn about the simple machine created in a bicycle shop in Dayton, Ohio.

Orville and his brother Wilbur had been asked to address the distinguished Western Society of Engineers on two different occasions. Officials from the United States, Great Britain, and France had met with the brothers about the possibility of purchasing Wright flying machines for their armies. These two former bicycle makers were now recognized the world over as the foremost authorities in aviation.

Now, undaunted by their own success, the brothers continued their work in the same humble fashion in which it was begun.

As Orville prepared for another test flight, the absence of swarming reporters offered a welcome reprieve. While the world was celebrating the dawn of aviation, the Wright brothers were diligently going about the task of improving the controls on their airplane. The original version had been completely cannibalized in favor of a new design intended to give the pilot more stability and control. A new engine was delivering almost twice the horsepower of the Flyer I. Several modifications had been made to the wings and stabilizers. And now Orville was anxious to measure their progress.

The engine sputtered to life, and soon the contraption was airborne. But within a matter of moments, it became obvious the modifications hadn't worked. After a few attempted maneuvers, Orville brought the craft back down, where it crash-landed, breaking four wing ribs. Once again, the brothers retreated to their workshop. Almost two years and a hundred test flights since the thrill of Kitty Hawk, there was still work to be done. As one biographer put it, "The Wright brothers had flown, but they still needed to learn how to fly."[5]

## GETTING OFF THE GROUND

Every day disillusioned Christians wake up to a new life that seems strangely similar to the old one. Where is the change? Where is the joy?

Where is the peace that passes all understanding? Unable to "mount up with wings like eagles" (Isaiah 40:31, NKJV), they grow confused, skeptical, and even uncertain about their salvation. Too often, people expect their Christian label to make them spiritually mature overnight. And when it doesn't, it causes them to doubt God, their faith, and themselves. These Christians have flown, but they still need to learn how to fly.

When we focus too narrowly on getting our "wings," it's easy to forget what Christianity is really all about: a lifelong process of being transformed into Christ's likeness. That initial experience of floating on air is just the beginning. The success of future flights depends on how well we prepare for them. While Christianity does change our eternal destination, it's no guarantee that our behavior here on earth will be altered.

We've all heard many testimonies of people whose lives were changed by Christ overnight. Criminals who leave their lives of crime to follow Jesus. Alcoholics who suddenly lose their desire to drink. Husbands and wives who pray "the prayer" and whose marriages are immediately healed. And while I would never doubt the authenticity of these accounts, I know for a fact that these are the exceptions, not the rule. God's timing is not the same for everyone. And for the majority of Christians, the transformation process is a slow, methodical one.

Unfortunately, we have a tendency to assume that if our spiritual experience is real, it will produce instant change. When it doesn't, we are prone to conclude that it didn't take. Or we think maybe we weren't sincere enough. Or we didn't have enough faith.

Here's a news flash for you: Being adopted into God's family does not necessarily, instantly, or automatically improve your character. The Bible doesn't promise sudden change. Spiritual growth comes as the result of a process called *renewal*.

## AN INTENTIONAL PROCESS

Let's take a careful look at Paul's instructions to the believers in Rome: "Do not be conformed to this world, but be transformed by the renewing of your mind" (Romans 12:2, NKJV). Imagine if Paul had stopped with the first part of the verse, "Do not be conformed to this world." While this is certainly an appropriate admonition, it isn't very helpful. This part of the verse simply restates what we've heard throughout our lives: "Be good." "Behave." "Get rid of those old habits." "Change!"

Maybe you're like me. I've never really struggled to know the difference between right and wrong—that part was generally easy. I knew *what* I was supposed to do, I just didn't have the *will* to do it. So how do we go about developing the will to do the right thing?

This is the point of tension in our pursuit of character. This is where the whole thing breaks down for most of us. Fortunately, Paul addresses it in the second part of the verse: "Be transformed by the renewing of your mind."

In other words, the means or vehicle by which transformation takes place is the renewing of the mind. Renewal is what transforms us.

Notice that Paul doesn't say, "Be transformed by rededicating your life." Nor does he talk about making promises to God, or feeling extra sorry, or praying a really long prayer, or filling out a card and joining the church. He doesn't mention any of the things we normally think of as catalysts for change.

Instead, you will be transformed by renewing your mind. This is the avenue leading to a changed life. It is the process that produces character.

If you are serious about becoming a man or woman of character, you must become intentional about renewing your mind. If you are not consciously attempting to renew your mind, you are not being proactive in your pursuit of character. Renewal is our part in the process. It's our way of working with the Holy Spirit as He molds and shapes us into the image of our Savior. *It is the most significant thing we can do to develop our character.*

You can spend the rest of your life making promises, filling out commitment cards, and talking to counselors. But Paul's words are very clear. Unless you renew your mind, you won't be transformed. Things will stay pretty much the way they are. Yes, you will go to heaven when you die. But in the meantime, you may not experience anything very abundant in this life.

Romans 12:2 is a powerful and revealing promise. It tells us that our transformation does not hinge on the depth of our commitment alone. This really is an interesting thought in light of the way commitment is heavily emphasized in most sermons and literature. If you think about it, however, the commitment to do something is nothing more than a sincere external gesture. Commitments are generally prompted by momentary emotion—a story, a testimony, a pang of guilt, a song. That's why so many people go back on their promises, give up on New Year's resolutions, and even abandon their marriage vows.

A commitment says nothing about what's inside a man or a woman. It doesn't necessarily represent the ability or even the dedication of an individual. Many promises are beyond the capability of the promiser. It is what's on the inside that ultimately determines what happens on the outside. This is why God doesn't ask for a commitment, but asks for renewal.

Christianity is not an event but a *process* designed with God's purposes in mind. Through renewal the wisdom and truth of God become the foundation of our thinking—and eventually our behavior. Over time a renewed mind results in a transformed life. Unless you are engaged in the process of renewing your mind, there will be no lasting improvement. Being a Christian doesn't guarantee change. Only a renewed mind does.

## THE ROLE OF UNDERSTANDING

The way you perceive reality serves as the foundation for all of your decisions. Your interpretation of the events around you serves as the basis for all of your attitudes. That's why renewal is such a vital part of change. In passage after passage throughout Scripture, the Bible addresses the subject of the mind, knowledge, and understanding. How we think is foundational to how we respond to everything—including God's law.

When we attempt to reconcile the commands of Scripture with thinking and attitudes that don't reflect reality, there is a conflict. I have a card on my desk at home that says, "Biblical imperatives apart from biblical thinking result in short-term obedience and long-term frustration."

Biblical commandments without the corresponding biblical worldview and understanding create a tension in our souls. There is conflict. God's commands don't make sense to us and don't fit our lifestyle. As a result, we aren't motivated to follow through. We experience a sense of powerlessness, and any well-intentioned efforts are short-lived.

If you don't believe me, ask the average Christian woman what she thinks about the notion of wives submitting to their husbands.

"Well, uh, I know it's in there…"

"But I think what he really means is…"

"The exception is…"

"And if a husband doesn't…"

The *what* is clear. But submission flies in the face of common sense—it just doesn't fit our culture.

But once a woman understands *why* God requires wives to submit to their husbands, it doesn't seem quite so ridiculous. In fact, it really makes a lot of sense. When a woman renews her mind to what is true about her, her husband, men in general, and the ways of God in marriage, then the command to submit is more easily received.

Ask the average single Christian male what he thinks about the notion that sex should be reserved only for marriage. Once again, you'll get a glazed look.

"I know it's in there, and it's probably a good idea, but…" But it really doesn't make any sense, does it? *Why* wait until marriage?

But when a man renews his mind to what is true of him, sex, marriage, and intimacy, suddenly God's law makes sense. It not only makes sense, it is compelling. But apart from biblical thinking, God's commandments regarding sex generally elicit short-term obedience and long-term frustration.

We often miss the *why* behind God's *what*. Discovering the *why* comes only through renewal. Spiritual maturity involves learning to see things from God's perspective. When we begin to interpret events, emotions, and relationships the way God does, our behavior eventually follows suit. When you see things from His perspective, His commands make sense. And your motivation to obey skyrockets. When we see as God sees, we are prone to do as He says.

## FROM FEAR TO FAITH

One of the added benefits of renewing your mind is that it increases your faith in God's love and concern for your life. As you renew your mind, you will understand more and more of why God has said the things He has said and required the things He requires. Along the way it will dawn on you that God's commandments are given as a line of defense against a world system that is designed to destroy you. God's law is given as a protective fence. Freedom is found within His moral and ethical will.

The more you come to accept the idea that God is trying to give you good things, the easier it becomes to obey His commandments—even when they don't seem practical. The more you encounter His faithfulness, the less you will doubt Him. Leaps of faith will feel more like a series of small steps.

For many believers, the Christian life feels like a never-ending routine of cliff jumping. God stands at the bottom of a dark hole and shouts, "Jump! Trust Me." To which they shout, "Why?" And God never answers. In fact, their fellow jumpers inform them that they aren't supposed to ask why.

Sure, in the initial stages of following Christ, there are some moments of decision that seem to parallel the cliff-jumping scenario. But after we've taken a few leaps of faith, we earn the privilege of looking back and seeing that the very commandments which once bewildered us were really some of the best advice we've ever taken.

Every summer, young children stand nervously at the edges of swimming pools while their fathers wait with open arms, pleading for them to jump. And every summer, the results are the same. Some children are overcome with fear and run back to Mom, only to wait another year to discover the joy of swimming. But some children stay. Carefully, they analyze the situation, looking for tangible reasons to believe it's okay to jump. But they don't know anything about swimming pools—or water, for that matter. Eventually, they realize that the only guarantee they have is the promise of their father.

And eventually that's all they need. And they jump.

At first it's a little scary. But after the initial splash subsides, they realize everything's all right. In fact, it was fun. So they ask to do it again. And again. And again. For the children who stick it out, this faith exercise not only leads to an afternoon of fun with Dad, but it also gives them more reasons to have confidence the next time Dad compels them to do something.

Your walk with God is similar. Like the patient father, God longs for you to enjoy the freedom you were designed for—and to enjoy Him. But our fear and lack of faith often prevent us from experiencing the good things He has prepared for us. God says, "Jump," knowing that safety is found in His arms, not on the side of the pool. But all we see is water. Unknown territory. We look around for a guarantee. Something to boost our confidence. And after searching, the only assurance we can find is the promise of His Word.

Some people walk away in fear.

Some step forward in faith.

The process of renewal is what gives us the ability to see that it's okay to jump. As we renew our minds, we learn about the pool. We learn about water. And most important, we learn about the arms that are reaching out to catch us.

## WHAT DO YOU THINK?

The best way to determine where renewal needs to take place in your life is to examine the way you respond to God's laws and principles for living. As we've seen, our natural tendency is to hear God's principles and edit them to fit our lifestyle. We rationalize our actions instead of conforming to His standard. It's human nature. A lot of it happens subconsciously. But if we stop and pay attention to our thoughts and emotions in these situations, we can learn a lot about our thinking. The following responses indicate a need for renewal:

- "Surely I'm not supposed to take the Bible literally."
- "I know I should put others first, but…"
- "I know he/she is not good for me, but…"
- "I know I should spend more time with my family, but…"

- "I know I should be more _____, but…"
- "I know I shouldn't watch that stuff, but…"
- "I know I don't have any business going there, but…"
- "I know what God says about money, but…"
- "I know I should forgive, but…"
- "I know I should be kind, but…"

When an issue arises, and the *what to do* is clear, but the *why to do* amounts to nothing more than "The Bible says…," then you have discovered an area of your life that needs renewal. You have discovered an area in which you are not convinced that God's way is best for you. You see God as standing in the way of what's best for you. Whenever that's the case, you are in serious need of renewal. Commitment won't cut it. And promising to do better will only result in your frustration. There's something about God's request that you don't understand. And if you ever hope to break free from the cycle of short-term obedience, then you need to find out what it is.

## THE POWER OF TEAMWORK

I'll never forget dressing our son Andrew when he was a newborn. Getting his little arms through shirt sleeves was like trying to catch fish with your bare hands. While I held the armhole open and took careful aim, his body would twist and squirm. I would make my move and he would bend in every direction but the right one. Eventually, one limb at a time, I managed to wrestle him into those little clothes. But it wasn't easy. He didn't understand the process. Actually, at that age, he didn't understand much of anything!

Then, little by little, Andrew began to catch on. Within just a few months he would see the shirt coming and lean his head toward it. Soon he was pushing his arms through the sleeves all by himself. As he got the hang of things, he made the job easier and easier. He knew what to expect; he knew where the whole thing was going.

Similarly, the process of developing character depends in part on your willingness to cooperate. God is trying to clothe you with His character. But if you don't understand what He's trying to accomplish, or why, you will likely make the process more difficult and more time-consuming. Like little babies, we often squirm and wriggle and resist what God is trying to do in our lives.

Good parent that He is, God consistently works to shape your character. And He is relentless. He loves you too much to let up or to give up. Since the day you were born, this has been His priority for your life. And it will continue right up until you take your last breath. But while God is faithfully working to produce character in you, oddly enough, much of your progress is dependent on your willingness to cooperate.

God's agenda for you is your character. What is your agenda for you? Is your priority for you the same as God's? Or do you give lip service to your relationship with Him, inviting Him into your decisions only when you desperately need help or when it fits your lifestyle?

Imagine your potential if you were to work *with* Him rather than working around Him. When the two of you are in alignment, there will be unleashed a whole new dimension of His power in your life. And as you renew your mind, you will begin to understand and cooperate with God's purposes for your life, rather than fighting against them.

# Chapter Eight

# Taking Off the Old

*Being confident of this, that he who began a good work*
*in you will carry it on to completion*
*until the day of Christ Jesus.*

PHILIPPIANS 1:6, NIV

The path seemed perfectly clear. From his vantage point on the beach, the young sailor watched as each vessel sailed out into the open sea, then disappeared over the horizon. He was convinced. The only thing that stood between Portugal and the wealth of the West Indies was a single body of water. And as he sat among the dunes, Christopher Columbus could barely contain his excitement.

There was just one problem. Everyone assumed that the world was flat. If a ship ventured out far enough, they believed, the ship and its crew would fall off the edge. So while the open sea beckoned, Columbus remained landlocked, imprisoned by the conventional wisdom of his day.

Columbus faced untold ridicule and hardship before he was granted permission to embark on his famous voyage. The journey itself was no less hostile. But while Columbus and his crew overcame tremendous challenges at sea, their adventure changed man's understanding of the world.

God is out to change your understanding of the world around you. Renewal is His method. Renewal is the process through which God looses us from the conventional lies of this world's system, and sets us free to enjoy the rewards of character.

Conventional wisdom tells us the world is flat. But that's a lie. Conventional wisdom tells us that cheating is okay, that compromising your integrity will pay off, that marriage is a trial-and-error endeavor, that there are no moral absolutes. But those are lies. Lies that keep us sailing close to shore. Lies that rob us of the opportunities that lie just beyond the horizon.

A renewed mind transforms a life in much the same way that Columbus's discovery transformed sailing. Columbus saw the error in the navigational assumption of his day, and he challenged that error with fact. Then he boarded his ship and acted on what he believed to be true. In doing so, he changed the trade industry forever.

Renewing our minds involves challenging the assumptions and beliefs that support our attitudes and worldview. It means identifying and facing up to errors in our thinking. And it involves replacing those erroneous ways of thinking with *truth*.

Renewing our minds is a two-part process:

1. Taking off the old.
2. Putting on the new.

In this chapter, we will examine the first step: taking off the old.

## OFF WITH THE OLD

When a woman paints her nails, the first thing she does is remove the old fingernail polish. Only then does she put on the new. When you refinish furniture, the first thing you do is take off the old finish. When an old car is repainted—if you're going to do the job right—the first step is to remove the old paint, sanding it down to the metal.

That's the process of renewal: Take off the old, and put on the new. The idea is to remove anything that will detract from a perfect new finish. When it comes to renewing the mind, taking off the old means identifying lies, wrong ideas, misperceptions, and misinterpretations that serve as the foundation of our beliefs and attitudes. In some cases, these are things we have believed all our lives.

Columbus grew up in a day when people believed the world was flat, and this miscalculation severely hindered his and every other sailor's potential. But then he went through a process of renewal, recognizing the error in the conventional wisdom of the day. He identified the truth, and then he acted on it. That is renewal in a nutshell.

The story of Columbus illustrates a very important principle:

*What we believe determines how we behave.*

This principle is foundational in understanding the importance of renewal. It functions as another avenue to explain the *why* behind the *what* of our actions. Every single facet of our behavior is somehow tied back to something we believe. When you and I believe the wrong thing, it works its way out in the form of wrong behavior.

The opposite is true as well. Right thinking paves the way to right behavior. This process is spelled out further in Paul's letter to the believers in Colossi:

> Do not lie to one another, since you laid aside the old self with its
> evil practices, and have put on the new self who is being renewed
> to a true knowledge according to the image of the One who cre-
> ated him.
>
> COLOSSIANS 3:9–10

We are to lay aside our old ways and put on the new. Command central for the renewal process is our minds, our thinking. Filling ourselves
with "true knowledge" entails dredging up and clearing out all the lies,
misinterpretations, beliefs that have no foundation in fact—anything that
is contrary to truth and reality.

## LIES, LIES, AND MORE LIES

We live in a world that lies to us every single day. All our lives, we have
been told lies. It's one of the consequences of living in a world that has
turned its back on the Source of truth.

Every day, women in our society are told in a thousand different ways
that in order to be lovable they must be beautiful. The message is that the
catalyst for lasting, fulfilling relationships is physical appearance. And
while few women would admit they buy into that line of thinking, fewer
still could deny having acted on it.

On the other hand, men are told that the key to their happiness is a
newer model that requires less maintenance. Whether the subject is cars or
women, the lie is the same. And it is a lie we see repeated every time we
turn on the television, open a magazine, or walk down the street. Once
again, I've never met a man who would acknowledge thinking that way.
But I know far too many who have made real-life decisions based on those
faulty presuppositions.

Repeated exposure to the lies of this world takes its toll. Over time, many of these lies get woven into the fabric of our thinking. We aren't always aware that they're there. In fact, often we are unaware of the ideas that form the basis of our decisions and attitudes. But these beliefs, whether grounded in reality or not, act as the grid system through which we interpret the data of our lives.

## MENTAL IMAGES

Your mental picture of God may be distorted because of subtle messages you received as a child. Maybe your picture of God is more like a picture of Santa Claus than the God described in Scripture. You see Him as a big, jolly figure who lives out in space somewhere. And as long as you're more nice than naughty, He'll be generous to you in the end. Or maybe you think God is a tyrant—no matter what you do, it will never be enough to quench His anger. Sure, He may "love" you because the Bible says He loves you, but He doesn't really *like* you.

To some degree, all of us live with distortions like these. Our perspectives are often skewed about marriage—about what a husband is supposed to be, about what a wife is supposed to do, about love, sex, money. And wherever there's a distortion of the truth, eventually it is reflected in our behavior.

If you believe the world is flat, you're not going to sail far from shore. If you believe happiness is found in the accumulation of possessions, you're not going to be very generous. If you believe that people cannot be trusted, you're not going to have many close friends. If you believe you are less than complete without a spouse, you're going to pursue marriage at a dangerously intense pace. If you believe you can't change, you won't. If you believe God accepts you on the basis of your performance, you're either going to perform yourself to death or give up altogether. And on and on it goes.

This is why you can promise, commit, and rededicate yourself over and over again without ever making any progress. Until you deal with your belief system, your behavior will never change. Because what we believe impacts what we do.

That being the case, *it is imperative that you begin identifying those things in your battery of beliefs that are not true.* The specific changes you would like to make in your behavior and character are linked to things you believe. No doubt you have already attempted to deal with these things at the behavioral level. And unless you have an extraordinary amount of resolve, you met with limited success.

But God's plan for change starts at the belief level. Your salvation began there, and your transformation begins there as well. Renewal requires daily, ongoing evaluation of your belief system. It doesn't happen all at once. Transformation is not a one-time event. It's a way of life. As you commit to the process, you will become sensitive to the assumptions that drive your behavior. In time you will become more discerning about the beliefs that drive your responses and reactions to the events of life.

## FIRST THINGS FIRST

You can't fill a glass with water if it's already full of dirt. You must first remove the dirt. You may use the water to help you do so. But either way, the dirt has to be removed before the glass can be filled with water.

In the same way, you can't fill a mind with truth until you have identified and removed the lies that reside there. A Christian can sit in church for years and listen to good, sound, application-oriented messages and never change. *You cannot fully embrace a truth until you have first removed the error that stands in contrast to that truth.*

A fellow who was having trouble in his marriage came to see me for advice. For forty-five minutes he told me all the things that were wrong with his wife. If half of what he said was true, he had every right to complain. He was a Christian, and he knew everything the Bible had to say about marriage. He was especially well-versed in the portions dealing with wives and submission.

When he finished, I asked him, "How can I help?"

"Tell me what I should do."

"What do you think God wants you to do?"

"I don't know. I've tried everything."

"What do you mean, you've tried everything?"

He went on to tell me all the things he had done to "help" his wife.

When he finished, I said, "I get the impression you want to 'fix' your wife."

"Yes," he said, "I do. But I don't know how."

As we talked further, it became evident that this biblically astute believer was operating from several false premises. Assumptions he wasn't even aware of. Assumptions that contradicted several passages of Scripture he firmly believed. But the truth of these passages never made their intended impact because of the undetected, covert lies that were warping his mindset.

*False Assumption #1: Husbands have been given the responsibility of fixing their wives.* That's what he actually believed. And since he believed that was true, he acted on it—which only made the problems worse. The truth is, God has not called men to fix their wives. He has commanded us to love them.

The interesting thing was that this man could *quote* the verse about husbands loving their wives. He knew it. He just wasn't operating from it. He said he had tried loving her. "I've tried being nice and sweet and patient, and nothing changed!" This brought to surface another false assumption.

*False Assumption #2: Love is a tool, and if it doesn't get the job done, it's okay to use another tool.* He tried loving her to get her to change. And when it didn't get the job done, he put down that tool and picked up another. But love isn't a means to an end. Manipulation is a means to an end. And when love is used as manipulation, it isn't love.

When being sweet didn't work, this man tried the opposite approach. He gave his wife a taste of her own medicine. He tried nagging and arguing and demanding his rights. He tried the silent treatment. And when he no longer enjoyed going home, he looked for opportunities to stay away.

*False Assumption #3: Rejection is the path to a restored relationship.* Another false assumption this man made was that his wife could be changed through repeated confrontation, fault-finding, and avoidance. He didn't know that's what he believed. On the contrary, he *thought* he believed that husbands are to love their wives like Christ loved the church. But that theological concept had never been internalized; it had never become part of his operational belief system.

Rejection never, never, never serves as a bridge back into a relationship. Yet many of us respond to rejection with more rejection. It comes naturally, but it doesn't work.

So I asked this man, "How does your heavenly Father go about changing you?"

He thought for a moment. "I'm not sure."

"Since you became a believer, has anything significant changed?"

"Sure, a lot."

"Did God ever nag you or shame you or reject you when you messed up?"

He knew where this was going. "No," he said.

"Do you know why God doesn't resort to that?" I asked.

He stared at the ceiling. "Because it doesn't work."

"Right."

We went on to talk about how love is the environment most conducive to change. I reiterated some of the false presuppositions he had been operating under. The longer we talked, the more misinformation we discovered. There were lies and false assumptions which he hadn't even been aware of. And they kept the truth he professed from sinking in at a functional level.

At the heart of almost every relational problem I have encountered are lies and false assumptions. The problem is never a lack of intelligence. Generally, it's not that the people I talk to aren't spiritually sensitive or committed to change. It almost always goes back to a faulty belief system.

And understandably so. Every time you open a magazine, every time you turn on a television, every time you have a conversation at work, every time you interface with any segment of this world, chances are you will be lied to. Over and over again, we are fed lies about what's real, about what's true, about how things work, about what's important, about what we "deserve," about how we ought to be treated. And unless we learn to recognize these distortions of the truth, we will inculcate them into our belief system and act accordingly.

Some of the lies we believe are very, very subtle. They're difficult to spot. To get you started, I want to share a few techniques to help you recognize the lies that have infiltrated your belief system.

One of the best ways to identify the false beliefs behind your behavior is by evaluating the things you say. You probably don't say these out loud, but you may think them. Statements like these are a good indication that there's some faulty thinking going on.

### 1. "I've always been this way."

"Well, I know I have a problem, but that's just the way I am. I mean, my father was that way. *His* father was that way. In fact, my whole family has always been this way. That's just the way I am."

Often we excuse shortfalls in our character by blaming our track record. We play the blame game. Rather than tackle the challenge of transformation, we choose to remain the same.

There are two false assumptions behind this idea. First, If I have been this way in the past, I must continue to be this way in the future. The second assumption is, My problem is more than God can handle.

When we point to the past to excuse our future, we are in effect saying to God, "I know You created the earth and the sun and the stars and six hundred different kinds of beetles, all the while observing the no-two-snowflakes-alike rule. I know You're the most powerful force in the universe. But God…I'm just too much for You to handle. I can't be changed."

I've never met anyone who would admit to such a pompous belief. But without recognizing it, many do believe it. The truth is, God has the power to overcome every flaw in our character, both known and unknown.

### 2. "Everybody else is doing it."

Assumption: *If everybody else is doing it, God doesn't take it as seriously.*
    "But I wasn't the only one."
    "Every attorney does it that way."
    "But everybody does their taxes like that."
    "The guy who passed me was going even faster."
    Behind each of these statements is the same lie. When we're caught

red-handed doing something wrong, we often fall back on this excuse, even if only subconsciously. When we attempt to justify our actions by comparing ourselves to others, we make a rather startling assumption: Whenever sin runs rampant, God becomes more tolerant. The more sin there is, the more He tolerates it. If enough people fall short of God's absolute standard of right and wrong, then He changes the evaluation system to a sliding scale, and everyone is graded on a curve.

Deep down, most of us understand that God's holiness would never allow for such a thing. Yet whenever we offer up the excuse that "everybody does it," we employ the belief that the quantity of participants in the sin impacts the severity of the sin. For a brief moment in time, our thinking is controlled by a false premise, and our behavior falls right in line with our thinking.

### 3. "I can handle it."

"What could it hurt? I can handle it." Another subtle yet damaging statement. The lie here is that if you can't see the harm in something, it must not be harmful. To adopt this belief is to say, "I'm discerning enough to know what's good for me and what's not. I don't need any outside input."

Of course, you would never openly say that, because anyone can see the fallacy of such a statement. But when we encounter it in subtler forms, we often miss it. And we believe the lie.

### 4. "One time won't hurt."

Other statements that might indicate you're believing a lie:
"I'll just try it once."
"It's just one party."
"I don't usually do this, but one time won't hurt."

Behind each of these statements is the belief that there are no consequences for sins that are committed only once. The implication is that
there are only consequences for repeated sins, habitual sins.

This lie is particularly devastating because of its subtlety. You
probably have certain goals you hope to reach in life, and along the way,
there will be many temptations to veer off course. Some will be obvious. But others will seem harmless. This lie suggests that certain
tangents are only temporary pit stops. And granted, the immediate
effects of "one time" sins may be minimal. But every habit has a first
time. Every detour begins with a small course adjustment. One time
*will* hurt.

### 5. "Nobody will know."

Another common lie is behind the rationale that says, "Nobody's going to
know." This is the lie that preys upon businessmen who travel alone. It's
the one that targets teenagers whose parents are out of town.

On the surface it ignores the fact that nobody is ever alone. And
beneath the surface, this statement assumes that as long as certain people
don't find out about our sin, then there are advantages that outweigh the
consequences. It says that God's standard of right and wrong is relative—
and that it only applies when someone else is watching. It suggests that the
only cost of compromise is the cost imposed by those who know and who
hold us accountable.

Like many of the other lies we believe, this one implies that the negative effects, if any, are short-lived. It indicates a belief that the only real
price of sin is the embarrassment and hassle of somebody finding out. But
as long as nobody knows…no problem!

6. *"But I'm in love."*

The toughest lies to neutralize are the ones linked to our emotions. The feelings associated with them can be so overwhelming that often we would rather believe the lie and suffer the consequences. In the heat of the moment, there's a sense in which we don't seem to care if it's a lie or not. But sooner or later the emotions pass. And when they do, we often look back and wonder, *What in the world was I thinking?*

Emotions are temporary. Consequences can last a lifetime.

When someone justifies sin on the basis of love, there is a serious belief problem. Love is the antithesis of sin. To justify sinning with someone because you love him or her is completely illogical. To introduce sin into a relationship is to sow the very seeds of its destruction. It would make more sense to say, "I know we shouldn't move in together, but I hate this relationship—I want it to end in grief, sorrow, and regret!"

Lust is a good rationalization for sin. Love is not. At the core of this statement is this assumption: Love is more important than obedience. That is, in the hierarchy of things, when it comes down to a choice between love or obedience, love wins out. But love for another person should never take priority over obedience to God. The truth is, obedience to God will enhance your ability to love others.

## FINDING THE LIES

In addition to examining the things we say, there are three other avenues for discovering erroneous assumptions.

*Closely examine the areas of your life where you are overly sensitive.* If there are subjects, names, or memories that create a sense of anxiety in you, then there may be a lie lurking beneath the surface. If you overreact to certain situations or when certain topics come up in conversation, it could be an indication of a false belief.

I have talked to husbands who feel like they're walking on eggshells because their wives are so sensitive about certain issues. That's usually a good indication that there's an area that needs to be examined. In some families, there are subjects that wives and children avoid mentioning around Dad because he'll overreact. That usually means there are areas that need exploring, where someone needs to ask, "God, have I believed a lie? Have I been set up?"

*Examine your strongest temptations.* Temptations are always camouflaged and supported with lies—it is the lie that makes it appealing. False assumptions make any temptation seem worth entertaining for the moment. Analyze your temptations. What exactly is the appeal? What is the promise of sin? What sort of mental gymnastics do you go through to justify it? Think through the conversations you have with yourself as you talk yourself into something you know is wrong. You will discover all kinds of things that you know are not true. But until the lies are exposed, it does little good to apply truth.

*Examine areas in which you have inordinate fears.* Of course, some degree of fear can be healthy. It's wise to avoid unnecessary dangers. But inordinate fears are those fears which are not grounded in reality. You know the facts, but you find yourself afraid anyway. Fear is often a sign that we are believing a lie.

One way to track down the false assumptions behind your fears is to play what I call the *What If?* game.

A lady says, "I'm afraid my husband will leave me."

I respond, "What if he did? What would happen?"

"I'd be alone."

"If you were alone, what would happen?"

"I'm not sure."

"So what exactly are you afraid of?"

"I guess I'm afraid of not being able to handle being alone."

"Have you ever been alone before?"

"Yes."

"How did you handle it then?"

"I did fine."

"Chances are, if your husband leaves, you will be fine."

This woman thought she was afraid of what her husband would do. In actuality, she was afraid of what she would do if her husband left her. When she discovered that, she identified a false assumption. Namely, "I can't handle being alone." That wasn't the case at all.

Once she was able to pinpoint the source of her fear, she was able to deal with it. In this particular case, she was able to overcome certain behavioral patterns that were actually driving her husband away. Her fear of abandonment was causing her to smother her spouse. He felt like she didn't trust him, when in fact, she didn't trust herself.

Renewal is a two-part process. It begins with identifying the lies and false assumptions that fuel our attitudes and actions. This is not a comfortable step. It can be threatening. But ultimately, it is liberating. Take some time to evaluate your excuses. Think through your temptations. Examine your fears. Ask the Holy Spirit to reveal to you the lies that hold you back in your pursuit of change.

God is at work in you. His goal is Christlikeness. His method is renewal. When you take steps to renew your mind, you are working hand in hand with your heavenly Father. And He has promised to complete what He has begun.

# Chapter Nine

# PUTTING ON THE NEW

*"Behold, I make all things new."*
REVELATION 21:5, NKJV

Taking off the old is only the first part of the renewal process. Just as we need to be intentional about discovering the lies we believe, so we need a deliberate plan for replacing those lies with truth. Lasting change is contingent upon both parts of the process.

"Putting on the new" begins where "taking off the old" leaves off. When scientists create a vaccine, they begin with the disease itself as a starting point. In the same way, to neutralize the lies that enslave us, we begin with the lies themselves. With the lies as our road map, or blueprint, we use them to lead us to the specific truth in Scripture that we will incorporate into the foundation of our new beliefs. And *specific* is the key word when it comes to putting on the new.

Once you identify an error in your belief system, the next step is to find its counterpart—the truth. This means finding the specific truths of God's Word that counter the specific lies you've been told. The goal is to equip yourself to the point that you have these Scriptures on the tip of your tongue. Then as you move through life and are confronted with lies, you'll be ready to counter them.

That's the process of renewing the mind.

It's countering lies with the truth.

## DIG A LITTLE DEEPER

Putting on the new often entails taking a different approach to the Bible. Finding the scriptural truths that apply to your particular situation will require some effort. And that means moving beyond a devotional approach to Scripture. It could mean opening your Bible on a daily basis for the first time. You will never renew your mind reading a couple of pages out of a devotional book and praying a prayer. Renewing your mind involves more than simply reading through the Bible in a year or answering your Bible study questions or filling out a workbook.

Bible studies and other programs can be great spiritual tools. But they can also give us a false sense of security. If we're not careful, we can look at all our books and study courses and cassettes and conclude that we are doing everything we can to become men and women of character.

I'm all for books, cassettes, and study courses. But I have seen too many "knowledgeable" believers wreck their lives over issues of character. If knowledge were the answer to spiritual maturity, we should all enroll in seminary. Knowledge does not necessarily result in a renewed mind. Knowledge has a tendency to puff us up and give us a false sense of spirituality. Satan knows a great deal about God. A lot of good that did *him!*

God wants to renew your mind with truth, not just fill it with facts.

Renewal hinges on specific truths appropriate for specific issues of character in our lives. The barriers that block and hinder our progress toward character must be identified and dealt with. Consequently, your pursuit of character will lead you beyond a devotional approach to Scripture. Renewal will involve digging out for yourself the specific biblical truths that counter the specific lies you have believed.

Christ demonstrated this process in a dramatic way immediately following His baptism. It is a familiar narrative, one used by preachers and teachers to illustrate just about everything under the sun. But more than anything else, it illustrates for us the amazing power of truth.

The story is found in Matthew's Gospel.

Jesus had fasted for forty days. *Forty days.* Over a *month* with no food. Imagine the shape He was in. In this weakened state, Satan came to Jesus with three tempting propositions, each wrapped around a false assumption.

Jesus, being God, could have looked at Satan and said something to the effect of, "Have you forgotten who you are talking to? I created you! Get off My mountain. For that matter, get off My planet."

But instead, Jesus took the opportunity to model for us the proper response to temptation and lies, temptation's supporting cast.

> Then Jesus was led by the Spirit into the desert to be tempted by the devil. After fasting forty days and forty nights, he was hungry. The tempter came to him and said, "If you are the Son of God, tell these stones to become bread."
>
> Jesus answered: "It is written: 'Man does not live on bread alone, but on every word that comes from the mouth of God.'"
>
> Then the devil took him to the holy city and had him stand on the highest point of the temple. "If you are the Son of God,"

he said, "throw yourself down. For it is written: 'He will command his angels concerning you, and they will lift you up in their hands, so that you will not strike your foot against a stone.'"

Jesus answered him, "It is also written: 'Do not put the Lord your God to the test.'"

Again, the devil took him to a very high mountain and showed him all the kingdoms of the world and their splendor. "All this I will give you," he said, "if you will bow down and worship me." Jesus said to him, "Away from me, Satan! For it is written: 'Worship the Lord your God, and serve him only.'"

MATTHEW 4:1–10, NIV

## ROUND ONE

In round one, Satan appeals to Jesus' depleted physical state and suggests He perform a seemingly harmless task: turning stones into bread. On the surface, this doesn't even appear to be a temptation. There was no Jewish prohibition against turning stones into bread. Jesus certainly didn't mind turning water into wine. So what was the problem?

The problem was that the Father had led Jesus into the desert. He was not there of His own accord. He was following instructions. And apparently His instructions included fasting until otherwise notified. The temptation was to put His own legitimate physical concerns ahead of His allegiance to the Father. Sound familiar? Is that not at the core of just about every temptation we encounter?

Shrouded in that innocent suggestion was a big lie. Namely, that satisfying your hunger is more important than devotion to the Father. But Jesus caught the lie and responded appropriately.

As I mentioned before, Jesus could have responded in several different ways. He could have said, "Well, you know, Satan, not only could I turn that stone into a piece of bread, I could turn *you* into a piece of bread! And so, I'm going to count to three…"

Instead, the first words out of His mouth were, "It is written…"

Not "I think…" or "I really shouldn't do that…" or "There's nothing wrong with…" The very first words out of Jesus' mouth were words of truth directed toward the specific lie hidden in that temptation. In this case, Jesus took a specific truth from the book of Deuteronomy that exposed Satan's lie for what it was. He said, "Man does not live on bread alone, but on every word that comes from the mouth of God." He was saying, "Life is not about eating; it's about faithfulness to My Father."

Satan was tempting Jesus to trade unbroken fellowship with the Father for physical nourishment, and Jesus recognized what was at stake. The issue was not rocks and hunger. The issue was loyalty.

That's our example. Truth for lies.

And it raises a challenging question. Have you filled your mind with enough "It is written" statements that you're prepared to combat the lies you face every day? When the world lies to you about what's important, do you have a ready response from God's Word? When the world says you have to be thin to be lovable or you need a certain amount of money to be respectable, do you know what to say? Is your mind so filled with "It is written" truths that as soon as you hear the lie, you can respond quickly with the truth? If not, then it is time to get busy.

If the Son of God felt it necessary to respond to Satan's specific lies with specific truths, what does that say about us? If anyone could have overcome Satan through sheer willpower, it was Jesus. If anyone could have reached down into his own reservoir of personal strength and experienced victory, it was Jesus. If anyone could have engaged Satan in a battle of wits and logic, He could.

But instead, He reached for truth.

And truth was enough.

## ROUND TWO

But Satan wasn't finished. He dared to enter the ring a second time. He took Jesus up on top of the temple and offered Him a chance to prove Himself to those below. And wouldn't you know it, he used the Scriptures to support his request, as if to say, "Okay, two can play that game." Don't miss the significance of that detail. Satan knows the Scriptures well. But knowledge is not enough.

Once again, there was a lie fueling this harmless request. I say "harmless" in that Jesus performed miracles throughout the Gospels to validate His message and identity. What would one more hurt? The problem here was not so much the *request* as it was the one making the request.

The lie was as follows: "Jesus, You have the authority to call Your own shots, don't You? You're a big boy. Do something on Your own for a change. It won't hurt. Besides, You're always doing this kind of thing."

But Jesus was a man under authority. On another occasion He made this clear when He said, "I tell you the truth, the Son can do nothing by himself; he can do only what he sees his Father doing, because whatever the Father does the Son also does" (John 5:19, NIV).

Satan knew that. That's why he appealed to the Father's promise of provision as a decoy in order to lure Jesus out on His own. But notice what Jesus does. Rather than engage in a theological debate about the true meaning of the passage that Satan quoted, He simply lays out another "It is written."

"It is also written: 'Do not put the Lord your God to the test.'"

Jesus exposes the lie, and He counters with the truth. That's renewal at its best. It goes beyond the realm of a token Bible study or devotional routine. Behind it all is a passion for character. A passion so strong that it fuels a deeper discipline and devotion to God's Word. And the result is a greater understanding of the whole counsel of God.

Interacting with the Scriptures at this level sensitizes our conscience to lies, half-truths, improper uses of Scripture, and misinterpretation of events. Filling your heart with the specific truths of God's Word prepares you for the daily onslaught of error. It will enable you to recognize the lies associated with the temptations continually hurled in your direction.

## THE FINAL ROUND

On the ropes and desperate, Satan went for a knockout blow. He took Jesus up to a high mountain and offered Him immediate control of all the kingdoms of the world. All He would have to do is bow His knee for a brief moment of worship.

Satan offered Jesus a shortcut. In effect, Satan was saying, "Okay Jesus, I'll make a deal with You. I know You came to earth to redeem the people of this world. And You know that at this moment this world is my kingdom. I'll trade You what You want for what I want. I'll trade You the kingdoms of this world for a moment of Your devotion. You can act as Lord of the nations, and I will be God. And this way, You won't have to wait. You can have it all now."

Apparently, Satan had the authority to hand Jesus the kingdoms of this world. Jesus never questioned him on that. What Satan was asking Jesus to do was to reshuffle His values.

So what was the lie? The lie was that redeeming the world was of greater value than devotion to the Father. Both were important. But one took precedence over the other. And so Jesus responded appropriately. Once again, right out of the Scriptures.

Jesus said to him, "Away from me, Satan! For it is written, 'Worship the Lord your God, and serve him only.'"

Satan offered a good thing. Jesus opted for the *best* thing. He saw the fallacy in Satan's logic. He recognized the lie hidden behind the offer of power. And He exposed it with the specific truth of God's Word.

## READY FOR BATTLE

How well are you equipped to combat the lies you face every day? When you are offered shortcuts, are you ready with an "It is written"? Do the responses pop right into your head and roll right off your tongue? Or do you stumble through these confrontations? "Okay, 'For God so loved...' No, wait. Okay, 'Now I lay me down to sleep...' No, that's not it..."

Chances are, you've memorized a few verses along the way. But are you equipped with the specific truths you need to combat the specific lies you encounter? What do you say when temptation stares you in the face? What about those areas where you're overly sensitive? Or those situations that strike fear in your heart? What do you say then?

We all know some general verses about God's love, temptation, sin, and fear. But do you have a specific verse ready for those areas where you're consistently under attack? This is how men and women are set free. This is where they're turned loose to reach their potential in Christ.

# Chapter Ten

# PUTTING IT ALL TOGETHER

*The integrity of the upright will guide them,*
*but the crookedness of the treacherous will destroy them.*
PROVERBS 11:3

As we have seen, transformation of character requires renewal of the mind, and renewal is a lifestyle. Therefore, some new habits are required. This may feel unnatural initially. Anytime we try something new, it feels somewhat uncomfortable, even intimidating. Remember turning on a computer for the first time? How about your first kiss? Think back to your first time behind the wheel of a car. What about your first experience lifting weights or trying to keep up in aerobics class?

After my first step aerobics class, my buddy and I went up to meet the teacher. There were about ninety people in the class, so I wanted to make sure he knew he had some newcomers. I introduced myself and told him that this was my first class. He smiled and said, "I know."

As you begin to apply the principles of renewal to your life, you may feel like the whole thing is too contrived to offer any authentic spiritual benefit. After all, it shouldn't be this complicated to become a person of character, should it? Shouldn't we just get better naturally because we want to?

Well, actually, no. When you take into account the world we live in, the families we grew up in, the pain we have experienced, and our propensity toward sin, there is a great deal of negative inertia we must overcome. Our natural drift is toward selfishness, not Christlikeness. To expect that you can drift effortlessly toward Christlikeness is tantamount to believing you could drift effortlessly up the Colorado river—it's not going to happen.

The good news is, it will only take one or two positive experiences with renewal to convince you that it's worth the effort. Learning to ride a bicycle is almost always a painful experience. Knees and elbows bear the marks of courage and determination. Ah, but that initial experience of freedom—that first solo flight of twenty or thirty yards—is enough to convince any kid that it will be worth the effort (and pain) in the end.

In the pages that follow, I am going to give you four practical tips to help you "put on the new." Remember, the goal of this step is to effectively counter the specific lies that have infiltrated your belief system.

## 1. SPEAK THE TRUTH OUT LOUD

I'm often asked, "Can the devil read our minds?" I don't think so. I can't read anyone's mind, but I can often guess what someone is thinking. The better you know someone, the easier it is to predict his thoughts and actions—as well as *influence* his thoughts and actions. The devil doesn't need to be able to read our minds to influence what we think.

For that reason, it is important to speak the truths of God's Word out loud. Jesus felt that it was necessary to say out loud, "It is written." He didn't look at the devil and meditate. He didn't try to stare Satan down. He spoke the truth right out loud: "It is written…" We would be wise to do the same.

You may feel a bit strange the first time you try this. But go for it anyway. Volume isn't the issue here. You don't have to shout it. Just say it.

Something powerful happens when we verbalize truth in the face of temptation or discouragement. Truth is powerful. Truth moves us beyond the realm of interpretation and assumption into the realm of reality. Truth takes our emotions and subjugates them to what is real.

Our feelings are wonderful followers, but they are terrible leaders.

This is why the Psalms are so powerful. There we find David's human interpretation of the events and circumstances surrounding him. We find there all the emotions that we would expect someone in his situation to feel. Then we read as David subjects his thoughts and fears to the test of truth. What is especially important to note is that he was not content to make this a mental exercise. As a musician, David had experienced the power of truth verbalized. By verbalizing his internal battle, he gained perspective and strength—he moved the battle from the internal world of subjectivity into the realm of objective reality. Sure, his enemies were all around him. Yes, there were times when all seemed lost. Yet in the midst of all of that, David writes:

> But as for me, I shall sing of Your strength;
>> Yes, I shall joyfully sing of Your lovingkindness in the morning,
> For You have been my stronghold
>> And a refuge in the day of my distress.
> O my strength, I will sing praises to You;
>> For God is my stronghold, the God who shows me lovingkindness.

PSALM 59:16–17

Verbalizing truth reshuffles our emotions. Truth frees us to feel *appropriately*—it casts a revealing light of reality on emotions that are stirred up by lies, misunderstandings, and inaccurate interpretations of the circumstances around us. It is hard to be honest if you are *afraid* of the outcome. It is difficult to be accountable if you are *worried* that someone might lose respect for you. Purity is difficult to maintain if you *feel* as if there are no consequences.

But spoken truth has a way of neutralizing misleading feelings. Truth deflates the swelling emotions that push us in self-destructive directions. Speaking the truth brings needed perspective to our panicking soul.

Sandra and I have a friend who grew up in a destructive home where she received almost no verbal affirmation. Needless to say, her self-esteem was in serious need of an overhaul. She became a Christian in her early forties. Slowly she began to accept the fact that her heavenly Father really did accept and love her. Unfortunately, this woman worked in an environment that reinforced most of what she heard growing up. Everything was negative. She was made to feel as if she couldn't do anything right. No praise. No gratitude. Just griping and complaining.

We tried unsuccessfully to help our friend find another job. And over time she resigned herself to the fact that God must have placed her there for a reason. Once she settled that issue, she began looking for ways to cope with the criticism. I suggested she think through what was being said about her at work to make sure there wasn't something she could do to improve her relationship with the people in her office. She came up with a couple of ideas, but nothing significant changed. Next, I had her write down the emotional messages her coworkers were sending her. An emotional message is what we *feel* someone is saying about us. This was her list:

"You're worthless."

"You're incompetent."

"You're stupid."

Every day was full of rejection. Add to this the scars from her past, and you can imagine the emotional shape this woman was in. But once she was able to identify and isolate the specific emotional messages she was receiving, she knew at once they were lies. She was mature enough in her faith to know that she wasn't worthless. She was overqualified for her job, so she knew she wasn't incompetent. And she would never have gotten her job to begin with if she had been stupid.

Realizing that these were all lies was helpful. But it wasn't enough. Next, she went to the Scriptures to dig out a handful of truths she could use to counter the untrustworthy messages she was receiving in daily doses. Here is a sampling of the verses she chose:

> But God demonstrates his own love for us in this: While we were still sinners, Christ died for us.
>
> ROMANS 5:8, NIV

> For you have been bought with a price: therefore glorify God in your body.
>
> 1 CORINTHIANS 6:20

> Therefore there is now no condemnation for those who are in Christ Jesus.
>
> ROMANS 8:1

> I will give thanks to You, for I am fearfully and wonderfully made; wonderful are Your works, and my soul knows it very well.
>
> PSALM 139:14

All day long she would say these verses out loud, just under her breath. Every time she was made to feel unworthy...*I have been bought with a price.* Every time she was made to feel stupid...*I am fearfully and won-derfully made.* When feelings of rejection welled up in her...*While I was still a sinner, Christ died for me.*

For three years, this was her daily routine. Nothing in her office envi-ronment changed. Nobody expressed appreciation for this woman's character and patience. But when God finally led her out, she was a differ-ent person. As I would listen to her share the details of what went on in her office, I would often wonder how I would have responded to so much criticism. I don't think I could have survived. And she would be the first to tell you that it was only through constant renewal that she was able to survive—and prosper. Such is the power of spoken truth.

## 2. PERSONALIZE THE TRUTH

This strategy for renewal involves quoting the truths of Scripture in the first person. For example, one of my character goals in life is purity. Just about every day I receive an emotional message that makes me feel as if I have no choice but to entertain whatever impure thoughts pop into my mind. The passage I have committed to memory to counter these feelings is from Paul's letter to the church in Corinth:

> We are destroying speculations and every lofty thing raised up against the knowledge of God, and we are taking every thought captive to the obedience of Christ.
>
> 2 CORINTHIANS 10:5

When I quote this verse, I put it in the first person. "I am destroying speculations and every lofty thing raised up against the knowledge of God, and I am taking every thought captive to the obedience of Christ."

This is a powerful verse. The term *speculation* can be readily applied to the "I wonder what it would be like" scenarios our minds are prone to latch onto.

I wonder what it would be like to be married to him?

I wonder what it would be like to try one of those?

I wonder what it would be like to watch that?

I wonder what it would be like to...

Another verse in my purity arsenal is found in Paul's letter to the church in Rome: "So then, brethren, we are under obligation, not to the flesh, to live according to the flesh" (Romans 8:12).

Again, when I quote this verse, I put it in the first person: "I am not under obligation to the flesh to live according to the flesh."

## 3. PRAY THE TRUTH

A third way to "put on the new" is to incorporate handpicked truths into your prayers. Another one of my lifelong character goals is loyalty, especially as it relates to my friends. One of my verses for loyalty focuses on what I say about other people:

> Let no unwholesome word proceed from your mouth, but only such a word as is good for edification according to the need of the moment, so that it will give grace to those who hear.
>
> EPHESIANS 4:29

Often I pray, "Lord, today it is my desire that no unwholesome word proceed out of my mouth. Let every word I speak be edifying according to the need of the moment that it may give grace to those who hear."

When you begin to incorporate these truths into your prayers, you're voicing your acceptance of the truth back to God. You're embracing the truth in His presence. Your prayers become an audible expression of your agreement with His plan for your character.

## 4. MEDITATE ON THE TRUTH

This is something my father taught me to do when I was very young. It's not something he suggested I do; instead, it was something I grew up hearing him talk about. He used to say, "Andy, the last thing I think about at night before I go to sleep is the truth." He would choose a verse or a part of a verse and rehearse it in his mind over and over until he fell asleep.

King David made this a part of his nightly ritual as well: "When I remember You on my bed, I meditate on You in the night watches" (Psalm 63:6).

Throughout the Psalms, David refers to the habit of meditation:

How blessed is the man who does not walk in the
    counsel of the wicked,
    Nor stand in the path of sinners,
Nor sit in the seat of scoffers!
    But his delight is in the law of the LORD,
And in His law he meditates day and night.

PSALM 1:1–2

Daytime meditation? If you're like me, you don't have much discretionary time to sit around and meditate on anything! Other than bedtime, the only consistent time I have to meditate is in the car. I write down my memory and meditation verses on little cards and put them somewhere on my dashboard. This has been my habit for eleven years. I have memorized dozens of verses while driving down the road. Some of my most helpful insights have come as a result of memorizing and meditating in the car.

## A PLACE TO BEGIN

This was not meant to be a "Four Steps to Successful Christian Living" chapter. These four suggestions are not steps to take. They are habits to develop, and that implies process.

Begin by developing your arsenal of verses. Then start committing them to memory. Now you might be thinking, *I can't memorize Scripture.* Guess what? You have just stumbled across a big lie that stands between you and the character you desire. "I can't memorize scripture" is a lie so common (and so absurd) that you would have thought we all would have recognized it for what it is a long time ago.

Of course you can memorize Scripture! You can memorize anything you want to memorize. In fact, you have memorized a lot of things you never intended to memorize. I walk around our house singing the Barney theme song all the time. You turn on the radio, hear one bar of music, and off you go—singing lyrics you never once sat down and made the effort to memorize.

The problem is not our ability or capacity for memorization. The problem is the *priority* we have given to memorizing Scripture. Granted, it's not the easiest task we will undertake, but it may very well be one of the most important. If you are going to put on the new, you need to have something new to put on.

Jesus stressed the importance of having something new to put on. He explained the process of renewal this way: "If you continue in My word, then you are truly disciples of Mine; and you will know the truth, and the truth will make you free" (John 8:31–32).

There's an equation in this passage that's so simple, and yet so profound.

*Immerse yourself in My teaching + Discover the truth = Be made free*

The word *continue,* or *abide,* is translated from a Greek word meaning *to remain* or *stay.* It is used in other places to refer to a specific geographic location. For example: "After this He went down to Capernaum, He and His mother and His brothers and His disciples; and they *stayed* there a few days" (John 2:12).

Jesus' point in John 8:32 is that His followers ought to stay, or remain, in His word. In the same way we would encourage someone on a diet to "stay with it," so Jesus exhorts us, "Don't give up. Don't grow weary. And don't drift away. Stay in My Word!"

If we remain in His word, we will "know the truth." Now, this is different from "hearing" the truth or being "told" the truth. And I don't believe Jesus is referring to one's general knowledge of the Bible. He does not promise that we will get any smarter. He promises freedom. And freedom comes when the specific truths of His Word cast a revealing light upon the lies that support our attitudes and emotions.

Of course, Jesus was talking about an internal freedom—being set free on the inside. The freedom He referred to does not depend on circumstances. He wasn't talking about being free from the Roman government. He wasn't talking about getting out of prison. He was talking about an *inside* freedom. He was promising the freedom to become everything God intended for you to be. The freedom to be molded and conformed to the image of Christ.

Remaining in His Word and discovering the truth removes obstacles between you and your character development. Truth paves the way for progress.

When I was in my midtwenties, it came to my attention that I had a habit of lying about my involvement in sports while in high school. When people would ask me if I played any sports in high school, I would always say, "Yes, I ran track and played soccer." Technically, that was true. While I was in high school, I did run around the track and I did play soccer. What I didn't say was that both of these activities took place during my PE class. I was never on either the soccer or track team at good ol' Tucker High.

Now, every time I told that lie, I felt terrible. But I could not bring myself to look at somebody in the eye and say, "No, I never participated in any team sports." This had been going on for years. I would promise myself I wouldn't do it again, but over and over again I would lie.

Finally, during my third year in seminary, of all places, something happened that forced me to deal with this character flaw. A friend of mine rushed up to me at church and said he had some great news. He told me he thought he could work it out for me to be the chaplain for the SMU football team.

My heart sank down into my socks. My friend was thrilled about this wonderful opportunity he had landed for me. And I felt like throwing up. That's when I knew I had a real problem. I knew there was a connection between my lying lips and my quivering knees.

After a week or so of real soul searching, I hit upon the root of my problem: I believed a lie. Somewhere along the way I had begun believing that to be a real, respectable, worthwhile man, I had to have accomplished something athletically.

Well-placed lies are powerful. They can chart our course for a lifetime if we let them. When I realized what had happened, I got busy replacing those lies with truth. In a short amount of time, I was free. Athletes no longer intimidated me, and I didn't feel compelled to lie about my athletic accomplishments. Before long, I could laugh about my lack of athletic prowess. Years later, I was invited to do a chapel service for the Atlanta Hawks. I remember walking into that room full of giants and thinking, *We've come a long way, haven't we, Lord?*

## YOUR PART, HIS PART

God is going to use a variety of things to shape your character. In most cases your only responsibility will be to trust Him and remain faithful. Renewal is the exception. The principle of renewal allows us to be proactive in our pursuit of character. It gives us a place to start. Renewal is our way of working alongside the Holy Spirit as He endeavors to conform our character to that of the Lord Jesus.

You know what you want to become. You have now surfaced some of the lies that stand in your way. Hopefully, you have started developing a list of verses that communicate the truths you need to focus on. Now start quoting them out loud. Personalize them. Pray through them. Turn off that radio and start meditating on them. And in the end, you will no longer be conformed to this world. You will be transformed.

# Chapter Eleven

# UNFINISHED BUSINESS

*In politics, as in life, it's better to be a skeleton
in a grave than to have one in your closet.*
ANONYMOUS

Directing our thoughts toward the future, the idea of *becoming* a man or woman of character allows us to take our eyes off what we are for the moment and focus them on what we hope to become. Suddenly, change seems like a real possibility. So we set our sights on tomorrow with every intention of putting the past behind us.

Unfortunately, it's not quite that simple. We can't really leave the past behind us until we have dealt with the unfinished business of the past. "Wait a minute," you protest, "becoming a man or woman of character is about the future, right? It's about what I do from this point forward, isn't it? There's nothing to be gained by poking around in the past."

But character development is not simply a matter of changing how you behave and think today. It also involves taking responsibility for how you behaved yesterday. At some point in your journey, God is going to call on you to turn and take responsibility for your past. Unresolved relationships, debts that have been neglected, apologies never made—these are things God will ask us to address. Chances are, you've said things you wish had never come out of your mouth, but once said, you never went back to apologize. All of us have people in our past whom we've hurt or offended. And many of those people still carry the wounds—wounds that a sincere apology would help to heal.

Part of becoming a man or woman of character is turning back and assuming responsibility for our past behavior. Often, moving forward means going back.

"Hold on," you say, "God has forgiven me. All things have become new in Christ. I'm a new creature. God gave me a brand-new beginning. I wasn't even a Christian when I did those things." Or perhaps you're thinking, *Yes, I was a Christian then, but I didn't know any better. Besides, that was a long time ago.*

Yes, God has made all things new. But that in no way relieves us of our responsibility to make things right with people we have mistreated. Character assumes the courage and the faith to do so.

## STOP THE SERVICE!

The importance of dealing with our past is one of Jesus' themes in His most famous sermon, the Sermon on the Mount. In this one public address, Jesus challenges the major tenets of His audience's belief system. One by one, He goes charging through all their misconceptions about God, worship, and even about their law.

And it is in this passage that we find instructions about how to deal with our past. What Jesus says about making things right may come as a shock to the modern reader, but it was even more astounding to the people of His day:

> "Therefore, if you are offering your gift at the altar and there remember that your brother has something against you, leave your gift there in front of the altar. First go and be reconciled to your brother; then come and offer your gift."
>
> MATTHEW 5:23–24, NIV

I can imagine someone in Jesus' audience thinking, *That can't be! I've walked all the way to the temple. I've stood in line for half the day. I've gone to all the trouble of finding an acceptable sacrifice. And You say I'm supposed to leave? God wants me to tie up my lamb or hand my pigeon off to someone else, just to make peace with someone who's mad at me?*

This was new territory. Worse than new, it was terribly inconvenient. And besides, it didn't make a whole lot of sense. The Jewish believers of that day believed their relationship with God was the ultimate priority. They assumed God would be more interested in worshipers making things right with Him than in making things right with someone else.

Perhaps you feel the same way. After all, aren't we to put God first in our lives? Isn't *He* supposed to be our priority? Certainly, we should be concerned about our relationship with others, but surely it can wait until after church!

But Jesus comes along in His characteristic fashion and reverses everything. In effect, He says our relationship with the heavenly Father *hinges* on our relationships with other people. The two are inseparable. He seems to imply that our ability to worship Him sincerely and fellowship with Him unashamedly is contingent upon our relationships with others—including those we have offended or hurt in some way.

The truth is, you cannot resolve your differences with the Father if you are unwilling to resolve your differences with others. You cannot be in fellowship with the Father and out of fellowship with others. The two go hand in hand.

## A NEW COMMANDMENT

The question that begs to be asked is, "Why can't God just forgive us and let us go on?" The answer to this is found in a statement Jesus made to His disciples during His final moments on earth: "A new commandment I give to you, that you love one another, even as I have loved you, that you also love one another" (John 13:34).

Remember what happened when a group of Jewish leaders asked Jesus which commandment was the most important in all of Jewish law? Jesus said that the entire law could be summed up in two statements: "'Love the Lord your God with all your heart and with all your soul and with all your mind and with all your strength.' The second is this: 'Love your neighbor as yourself.' There is no commandment greater than these" (Mark 12:30–31, NIV).

The practical side of character is all about loving others. The Christian faith is built on the premise of *others first*. After all, that's how people are going to know we are Christians; it is our love for one another. The greatest evangelistic tool we have is love. Love for other believers and love for those outside the faith.

It is impossible to be right with God while neglecting this important command. There is something insincere about a man or woman who repeatedly tells God how much he or she loves Him while refusing to obey Him. To love God is to keep His commands, and He has commanded us to love. You cannot love God with all your heart and not love your neighbor; the two are inseparable. And by the way, it doesn't stop with loving our friends and neighbors. Jesus went so far as to say we are to love our enemies (see Luke 6:27).

It goes without saying that the type of love Jesus is talking about has nothing to do with how we *feel*. After all, we certainly can't be expected to feel loving toward an enemy. This is a "do" kind of love. The issue here is how we treat our neighbor—and how we treat our enemy. We are commanded to say and do things that demonstrate love. And when we don't, it affects our fellowship with the Father.

## GRACE MISAPPLIED

Part of our confusion in this area stems from a misapplication of grace. When you became a Christian, you came face-to-face with the unconditional, undeserved grace of God. If you were like me, it was an overwhelming thing to realize that there was nothing you could do to earn your forgiveness or salvation. It was a gift. Period. Nothing you had done had any merit. Your good deeds did not, and could not, earn you good standing with God.

Now that may be true of your relationship with God. But it is *not* true of your relationship with others. God has forgiven you—but those you have wronged in the past may not have. In fact, they may very well be hostages to bitterness and anger over what you did to them. We're kidding ourselves if we think that everybody we have ever wronged has simply forgiven us and gone on with life. Sure, that's what they ought to do. But if we always did what we ought to do, forgiveness wouldn't be an issue with us in the first place!

We're kidding ourselves, as well, if we think we have no responsibility for making restitution. The grace that was showered on us at salvation did not provide us with an escape hatch from our responsibility to others. On the contrary, that very grace should *compel* us to make restitution with those we've wronged. Christ paid a debt He did not owe and one we could not pay. That kind of love should motivate us to pay those debts we can pay.

The penalty for our sin, insofar as heaven and hell are concerned, has been dealt with once and for all. The consequences of our sins are a different matter altogether. We are avoiding the clear teaching of Scripture if we are using our forgiveness as an excuse to avoid the pain and embarrassment of reconciling with others. It is true that you can never repay God for all He's done for you. But you may certainly be able to repay your fellow man for what you have done to *him.*

Nobody seemed to catch on to this concept more quickly and thoroughly than Zacchaeus. We usually have a cute picture in our minds when we think of Zacchaeus, the tax collector whose story is told in Luke 19. He was the "wee little man" who climbed the tree because he couldn't see Jesus over the crowd. But Zacchaeus had been a wicked man who had wronged many people. But when Jesus invited Himself to dinner at Zacchaeus's house that day, the little tax collector was changed forever. Jesus loved him in spite of his wicked past, and he was given a clean slate.

Zacchaeus was so moved by his encounter with Jesus that he decided to give half of his goods to the poor. And that was just for starters. Then he said, "I'm going back to everyone I've ever robbed. And not only am I going to give back the money I stole, I'm going to give them four times the amount I took."

Did Jesus say, "Oh no, no, no, Zacchaeus! You're forgiven. You see, old things have passed away. Behold, all things have become new. You just need to move on from here. You don't have to worry about the past"?

No. Instead, Jesus affirmed Zacchaeus's decision to take responsibility for what he had done in the past. Zacchaeus understood that following

Christ wasn't just about *now*. And it wasn't just about the future. It involved taking responsibility for his past, too.

## MOVING ON

So you see, pursuing Christlike character may entail a trip down memory lane. It may mean going back in order to move ahead. From time to time your heavenly Father may require you to leave your sacrifice and go deal with an unresolved relationship. You may have to make an awkward phone call or two, set up an appointment, or write a long overdue letter.

Now I'm assuming this is not your favorite chapter. You may have picked up this book in search of truths and principles that will help you put the past where it belongs, behind you. The very notion of dredging up the past is probably enough to make you want to reach for the newspaper or see what's on TV, but I hope you won't. I hope you will allow God to finish what He has begun in you—even if it is painful.

Reconciling relationships and making restitution are what men and women of character do. These are signs of spiritual maturity and personal security. Sure, it is inconvenient. Yes, it is embarrassing. Often, it is humiliating. But remember: Your Savior suffered a painful, inconvenient, and terribly humiliating death on a Roman cross for the sake of past and future sins that He didn't even commit. He took responsibility for the sins of the whole world. He died so that you and I could be reconciled to the Father.

Let's face it, in the shadow of the Cross all our excuses, all our griping, all our rationalizations amount to nothing. We really have no excuse. His reconciling death was for our good, and His instruction to us regarding our responsibility to reconcile with others is for our good. To say no to Him now is to resist the love of the One who has shown in unmistakable ways that He has your best interests in mind.

Perhaps you have an ex-wife or ex-husband who repeatedly rakes you over the coals about the same issues, most of which are ancient history in your mind. But as you listen, you know that one of those issues really *does* belong in your court; you are partially to blame. And it could be that this is something you've never really owned up to.

Or maybe on your way out of your former place of employment you took some things that didn't belong to you. You justified it by the mistreatment you experienced there. Or you had a business associate, and one day you lost your temper and said some really nasty things. And everyone who heard it knows you're a Christian. But you've never gone back to apologize.

These are the kinds of things that your Father will more than likely bring to your attention. Not to condemn you. Not for the purpose of loading you up with guilt. No. His purpose is to give you an opportunity to do the right thing, even when it is hard. Even when it costs you something. After all, that is the nature of character.

Of course, you don't have to follow through. God is not going to put a leash around your neck and drag you into submission. There are always alternatives. But there are some stiff consequences associated with disobedience in this area.

## CONSEQUENCES

When you ignore God's promptings to reconcile, it has an automatic impact on the sincerity of your worship and service. You are covering something up. You have put up an "off limits" sign on an area of your life. You cannot withhold an area of your life and worship God sincerely. You cannot be the kind of worshiper He seeks while refusing to deal with the issues of reconciliation and restitution.

Insincere worship results in a subtle shift from relationship to ritual.

You will go through the motions, because that's what you are supposed to do. But there will be something missing. Whenever we put up an "off limits" sign, our worship and service become superficial. We replace fellowship with activity, routine, and attendance.

Refusing to deal with our past will eventually impact current and future relationships as well. I see this all the time in second marriages. When a man or woman moves into a new marriage without first owning up to his or her share of the failure in a previous marriage, there is always a price to pay.

Intimacy is always an issue in this scenario. Unresolved relational conflicts impact our ability to experience genuine intimacy, and our tendency is to blame the problem on current relationships rather than take responsibility for past ones.

Guilt from past unresolved relationships often finds its way into current relationships. When we spend years refusing to take responsibility for something in our past, we often become emotionally detached. This detachment often creates a wall between us and those we love the most.

When we harbor sin, we continually have to cover for ourselves. Our subconscious mind is always at work covering up, while avoiding the people or situations that could blow our cover. After all, what would happen if people knew? What if they found out? So we hide. And the walls of protection we develop to keep our past in, keeps others out. Tragically, it is often those we love the most that feel the full weight of our isolation.

## "I HAD A CHRISTIAN FRIEND ONCE..."

One major consequence of leaving old business unfinished is that it misrepresents God to those outside the faith. Many unbelievers have chosen to remain so because they knew, did business with, or lived next door to people who were Christians. And the whole experience left a bad taste in their mouths.

When a believer harms an unbeliever in any way, and never comes back to assume responsibility for his or her behavior, the consequences can have eternal ramifications. I have met scores of non-Christians who are quick to blame their unbelief on their interaction with another Christian. Granted, those stories are generally smokescreens for a different issue. But it's a shame that they would even have those stories to tell.

Reconciliation is not limited to our brothers and sisters in the faith. It may be even more important to apply this teaching to those who are *not* in the faith. Asking forgiveness and reconciling relationships is at the heart of the gospel. What better way to demonstrate and illustrate our message.

But perhaps the worst consequence of our unwillingness to own up to our responsibility is that it often fuels the fires of bitterness and anger in someone else's life. For many who have been hurt and whose souls are filled with the self-destructive fury of anger, a word of apology or acknowledgment could set them free.

All they would need to be released from the eroding forces of bitterness is for the one who has hurt them to go to them and make it right. To say to them, "I know I could never repay you fully. I know I can't make this go away, but I'm here to let you know, I'm responsible and I'm sorry. And if there's something I can do about it, I'm willing to do it."

## TURN IT AROUND

If you want to know how much of an impact this can have, turn it around. Just imagine how you would feel if you got a surprise visit from someone in your past who had hurt you and never made it right. Think for a moment about someone who has wounded you deeply and has never come to you to apologize. How would you feel if that individual walked in, sat down, and took full responsibility for what he or she did?

Maybe it would be your dad calling to say, "I know I'll never be able to make up to you what I've taken from you as a father. But I want you to know I'm sorry. Would you please forgive me?" It could be a former boss, or an employee who quit and then trashed your name throughout your industry. It may be somebody that you've always avoided because of how angry that person made you. How would it affect you if that man or woman looked you up and apologized?

No wonder God has called us to take responsibility for our past. Doing so brings healing and wholeness to wounded souls. Think about it: If someone you knew had that potential and refused to exercise it simply because it is temporarily awkward and embarrassing, what would you think about that refusal? Wouldn't that reflect poorly on that person's...character?

God's forgiveness does not exempt you from exercising your responsibility. On the contrary, His forgiveness is *the* reason to take it to heart. God paid a high price to reconcile you back to Him. And now He's calling on you to pay the price to reconcile yourself to others.

Several years ago I was preaching for my dad while he was out of town. And of all the topics I could have been preaching on, I was talking about being blameless. I remember saying something like, "If you are truly blameless, then you can stand up to any scrutiny. The president could ask you to be the attorney general, and you'd sail through the confirmation hearings without a glitch because your record was clean." And just as I said that, it was like God thumped me on the back of the head and brought an unresolved relationship to my mind. Actually, it wasn't the first time He had reminded me of this particular incident. About every three or four months I would get a gentle reminder. But this wasn't all that gentle. I almost lost my train of thought right in the middle of the sermon. I remember thinking, *Lord, this is not the time!*

I made it through the sermon and then went back into my dad's office to have my usual song-and-dance prayer with God to get Him off my back. And as usual, the conviction went away. But not for long.

A few days later, I was having my quiet time, and I couldn't pray. All I could think about was this man that I knew God wanted me to straighten things out with. I tried to resist it. Finally I said, "Okay God, You've forgiven me. Now I want to pray for Sandra and the kids...." But that didn't work. It was like God was saying, "Andy, you're not blameless. You're hiding something." And I remember thinking, *But it's complicated, and it was so long ago, and it is probably no big deal by now....* And on and on I went. But the impression was so strong. I finally concluded that it would be a lot easier to deal with it than to continue arguing with God.

So I got in my car without the slightest idea what I was going to do. I just had to make things right with this fellow and his family. So I drove to his house. Then I drove past his house. Then I drove past his house again. It took me a long time to get up the nerve to stop. I can't recall another time in my adult life when I've been so nervous about something. I didn't know if he'd be angry, or if he'd just think I was crazy. For all I knew, he would call the police.

Finally, I parked in the driveway, walked up to the door, and rang the doorbell—hoping nobody would answer. But the man came to the door and looked at me with the most confused look you can imagine. And rightly so. I had never been to his house before. We were never close friends. And I hadn't seen him in years.

"Andy? What in the world are you doing way out here? Come on in."

I was dying. He didn't have a clue why I was there. Which meant he didn't know what I had done. Otherwise, he would have thrown me off his property—or so I thought.

As soon as I sat down, I blurted out, "I've come to apologize." And he just stared at me. He still didn't know. So I said it again. Primarily because I was afraid if I didn't just start, I would lose my nerve. I told him what I had done. And I told him how sorry I was. He kept staring at me. If he had stood up and knocked me across the room, I think I would have felt 100 percent better. I certainly deserved it. So I told him that, too. Any response from him was totally justified in my mind.

When I finished, he smiled and said, "You know, I had a feeling it was you."

Now you have to understand, I had carried this for years. And all along, this person had a hunch that I was behind an event that had caused him a great deal of pain and expense. As long as I live, I'll never forget what this gentleman said at the end of our conversation. He looked at me and said, "Andy, this makes me feel good all over." I saw release in his eyes. The healing process was complete. We all had a good cry, and I left.

For someone in this world, you may hold the last piece of a puzzle he or she has been attempting to complete for a long time. This individual has tried to forgive—tried to move past what happened. But your owning up to your responsibility may be the thing that allows this man or woman to really move on with life. But even if that is not the case, Jesus says, "Go and be reconciled to your brother."

Character is as much about the past as it is the present and future. Your past relationships cast an inescapable shadow over your fellowship with the Father. Before you seek to take another step in God's direction, it could be that you need to take a step of reconciliation toward someone else. Maybe the time has come to make that call, write that letter, visit that old acquaintance. And as you step out in faith and humility, know that in doing so you may be unlocking the gate that leads to healing for both you and the one you wronged. Your going back may be the very thing that sets you and others free to move ahead.

# Chapter Twelve

# LETTING GO
# OF THE PAST

*The right response can take the most painful
memory and make it a blessing.
The wrong response can end up being very destructive.*
<small>DR. CHARLES F. STANLEY</small>

I t appeared that Paris, the son of King Priam, had endured the siege. The dusty battlefields surrounding the city walls were empty. After several days of intense fighting, Troy had stood her ground. Unable to break through the Trojans' perimeter defense, the last of the retreating Greeks could now be seen boarding their ships in the distance and heading out to sea. All the citizens breathed a sigh of relief.

As the soldiers stood atop the fortress, surveying the damage, their eyes were drawn to a strange object that stood outside the entrance to the city. Curiosity spread throughout the ranks as the people huddled in turrets and around portal windows to see what appeared to be the figure of a large animal. But what did it mean?

The High Council held a meeting to consider the matter. After some deliberation, they concluded that the defeated Greeks had left behind the large wooden horse as a gift to symbolize their full surrender to a superior foe. It was a suitable gesture, considering the casualties Troy had endured. The Greeks' visit had come at great expense to the Trojan army and its citizens; they were entitled to some token of restitution. The horse was rightfully theirs.

The city gates were opened. A garrison of soldiers was dispatched to wheel the horse inside. Its workmanship was fine. The people gathered around to admire the artistry of their new trophy. It would make a stately monument to commemorate this long-awaited moment of victory. Within the safety of the city walls, a great celebration broke out. The people danced and feasted late into the night, until their exhaustion brought peaceful sleep to the city.

Then, under the cover of night, the plot was revealed. In the silence of the early dawn, the wooden horse stirred to life. Beneath the creature, a secret door swung open. Slowly, a human head peered out. The coast was clear. One by one, a squad of Greek soldiers emerged from inside the horse and disappeared into the shadows of Troy. Each took his assigned position and readied for the attack. In the meantime, the entire Greek fleet had quietly returned, and the Greek army once again encircled the unsuspecting city in full force. At a given signal, the hidden soldiers flung open the city gates, and the attacking Greeks marched in without resistance. A great slaughter ensued. Many of the Trojan women, including members of the royal family, were carried off into captivity. Troy was ruined. The same horse that had stood as their monument of victory had become the instrument of their defeat.

# THE PLOT TO CONQUER YOUR HEART

A Trojan horse sits just outside the gate of your heart. Its name is *bitterness*. It is a monument to every attack you have endured from your fellow man. It is a gift left by the people who have wronged you. It is a monument to the pain, sorrow, and devastation they have caused you. It represents the debt they will owe you until the day they are brought to justice. It is rightfully yours.

But to accept the gift is to invite ruin into your life. You see, there's more to the horse than meets the eye. The feeling of justification it brings is the deceptive artistry of a master craftsman. Though decorated with the promise of vindication, it is only a lure. The celebration is short-lived. Once inside the walls of your heart, it releases its agents of destruction. Its plot quietly unfolds from the inside out. To become a person of character, you must learn to recognize the Trojan horse of bitterness. And more important, you must never bring it inside.

Owning up to your past is an important step toward developing character. As we've seen, in order to keep a growing, honest relationship with God, you need to take responsibility for the people you've hurt. *But what about the people who have hurt you?* Chances are, the fallout from these painful interchanges will create an even greater obstacle in your pursuit of character.

Unresolved hurt opens the gate of our heart to the destructive forces of anger, resentment, and bitterness. And nothing so retards the growth of character as these three things. They are hindrances that no amount of dedication and determination can counteract. They must be dealt with, not compensated for.

And the only remedy is forgiveness.

Hurt, rejection, abandonment, and abuse leave us feeling like victims. It is the feeling of victimization that enables the harm inflicted on us by others to become an obstacle in our pursuit of character. Victims are powerless. Victims have no control over their lives. Victims are at the mercy of others. Victims can only react. Victims are prisoners. A victim has an excuse. A victim can excuse just about any kind of behavior. After all, look at the way he's been treated. Look at what she's had to endure. What should we expect from someone who has suffered like that? And so pain and hurt create an unscalable wall of excuses and rationalization.

To make matters worse, the current trend in psychology is to place more and more of the blame for our nation's character deficit on our culture. Individuals are no longer responsible for their decisions and behavior because, it is said, individuals are nothing more than by-products of our society. They had no choice in how they were brought up. Consequently, individuals are not to blame for the choices they make. Collectively, we are all to blame. And individually, we are all victims!

The message is, "It's okay for you to behave the way you do. You have no choice in light of your background. For you, this behavior is perfectly acceptable. You are under no obligation to change. You have every right to be the way you are." Such thinking removes all incentive to change. After all, it's always easier to stay the same and make excuses. Victims don't want to be proactive about changing. Instead, they want to be proactive about making sure that the person who hurt them pays. And so we spend our energy telling our sad stories rather than tackling the task of forgiving.

In doing so, we open the doors of our hearts and welcome the Trojan horse of bitterness. It becomes a monument. It stands there as a constant reminder of a debt someone has yet to pay.

# FORGIVE AND FORGET?

Remember, your character is always either improving or deteriorating. It is either getting better or worse. Nothing contributes to the deterioration of character like unresolved hurt. Bitterness is like a cancer, attacking every healthy thing it contacts. And so your character deficiencies will eventually make contact with the healthy relationships in your life.

Bitterness cannot be contained. It always spreads. Forgiveness is not optional. Relationally speaking, it is a matter of life and death.

So what are we saying here? Forgive and forget? In fact, true forgiveness is more about remembering than forgetting. It involves facing the past, not suppressing it.

When you are not the victim, it's easy to give pat solutions for the pain someone else is feeling. And it's easy to take a quick look at a few Bible verses and conclude that the solution is just to "forgive and forget." But our minds don't have a delete button. Memories don't die easily.

As a pastor, I spend a good bit of time listening to stories of hurt, abuse, and injustice. I can appreciate the sense of helplessness people feel when they have been taken advantage of by someone they trusted. In my heart, I often wonder along with them, *God, how could You allow such things to happen?* I can relate to their desire for justice. Retribution. Payback! And often I am hesitant to say to people, "Forgive. Just forgive! Let it go. Put it behind you. Move on with your life." It sounds so insensitive. So pat. So trite. Forgiveness seems like such an oversimplification at times. Besides, what if they're in a situation where there are repeated rounds of abuse and rejection? When is enough, enough? How many times does God expect us to keep forgiving the same person for the same thing? There's got to be a limit—or so conventional wisdom tells us.

My hesitancy to exhort people to forgive, and the question of "When is enough, enough?" are fueled by a common misunderstanding about the nature of forgiveness, one that hangs people up for years in their pursuit of character: We have a tendency to view forgiveness as a gift to the one who offended us—as a benefit to that person. For this reason, we are hesitant to forgive. Why give something to someone who has already taken something from us? That doesn't make any sense. After all, *we* are the ones who are owed.

But as we're about to see, forgiveness is not a gift for someone else. Sure, it may involve granting a pardon for an offense. But that's just the beginning. The effects of forgiveness run much deeper. For the most part, it's a gift that was designed for us. *It's something we give ourselves.* Because when you consider everything that's at stake, the one who benefits the most from forgiveness is the one who grants it, not the one who receives it.

## THE RIGHT QUESTIONS

We are not the first generation of believers to grapple with the question of, "When is enough, enough?" We are not the first to wonder if forgiveness is always appropriate. The apostle Peter had the same question.

One day Jesus was explaining how to deal with some rather complicated relational issues. Peter was listening intently. The whole dialogue reminded him of something going on in his own life. Apparently, Peter was in a relationship with someone who was repeatedly offending him. He had heard Jesus talk about forgiveness before. He understood his responsibility to forgive. But he wasn't sure how far to take it. So Peter pulled Jesus aside and asked Him, "How often shall my brother sin against me and I forgive him? Up to seven times?" (Matthew 18:21).

In other words, "When is enough, enough? How many times do I have to forgive? Is it always appropriate to forgive?" Peter wanted to do the right thing. But come on, we all have our limits. Where is the justice in a system where forgiveness is offered at every turn?

Knowing that Jesus expected more than the average teacher, he took a stab at what he believed would be a generous answer. "What about seven times?" Peter was catching on. No doubt there was a time in Peter's life when he would have suggested two times or, possibly, one. But he had been listening. He knew that Jesus' perspective on things was different than that of the religious teachers. But when it came to forgiveness, Peter didn't grasp just how different it really was.

By asking, "How often shall I forgive?" Peter revealed his misunderstanding about the nature of forgiveness. Like us, Peter assumed that forgiveness is for the benefit of the offender. And like many well-meaning Christians, Peter was willing to stretch, willing to be a nice guy. He was willing to go seven rounds with the same person over the same issue. But after that—or after some other predetermined point—no more forgiveness.

Of course, you can't blame Peter for thinking that way. After all, when people hurt us, when people do something malicious to us, there is a sense in which they have taken something from us. They have stolen from us. They become indebted to us. They create a deficit in the relationship. That's why we say things like "You *owe* me an apology" or "I'm going to get *even* with him."

Things are out of balance. And in order to achieve justice, a transaction must take place that transfers something back to the victim. It could be an apology, a favor, or some other form of restitution. For example, if somebody gossips about you, it amounts to stealing your good reputation. When an adult abuses a child, it's the same thing as stealing that child's future ability to trust. When a wife runs around on her husband, she steals a piece of her husband's self-esteem. When an employer fires an employee unjustly, the employer steals the employee's financial security. And on and on we could go. Whenever there is hurt, there is thievery. There is an imbalance. Somebody owes someone. And who will pay that debt?

People who have been robbed emotionally are generally looking for two things. First, they want recognition and affirmation that they were, indeed, the victim of a crime. Second, they want the perpetrator to replace what was taken. Unfortunately, there are significant problems with both of these objectives. In almost every case, one or both of these goals are unattainable. In some cases the victim may get unanimous public affirmation that the crime took place. But that is rare. Even more rare is a situation where a victim is paid back for what is taken. In the vast majority of cases, what was taken can never be replaced. The perpetrator couldn't pay it all back if he wanted to. Something is gone forever.

You can't pay back a relationship. You can't pay back lost time. You can't pay back a reputation. There is no way to make up for years of criticism and neglect. The truth is, nothing can make up for the past. There is an emotional element involved in hurt that cannot be compensated for through apologies, promises, or financial restitution. To some degree there will always be an outstanding debt.

To pursue payback is futile. It can't be done. To sit and wait for an apology and restitution is to set ourselves up for failure and further disappointment. For while we are waiting, the seeds of bitterness take root. And what begins as a holding pattern becomes a vicious cycle. Hurt people who hold on to their hurt, waiting to be paid back, always hurt other people. Victims become victimizers. We do to others what others have done to us. Along the way, we lose the will to do what is right.

Pain sets us up to become self-centered. The more intense the pain, the more self-centered we tend to be. Think about the last time you experienced a serious physical injury. On whom did you focus? What was your greatest concern at the moment? *You.* That's the nature of pain. It's difficult to give your attention to anyone or anything else.

Emotional pain works the same way. And like physical pain, the more intense the emotional pain, the more self-centered we become, and self-centeredness is the archenemy of character. Men and women of character are committed to putting *others* first. The golden rule is the standard. Consequently, holding on to hurt sidelines a man or woman in the pursuit of character. It short-circuits the whole process.

## PROTECTING THE WOUNDS

I see this cause-and-effect relationship working itself out in marriages all the time. A couple will come in, both parties full of anger and each complaining of multiple hurts and offenses. So I say, "Well this is easy. Just forgive each other and go on with your lives."

"Well, it's not that easy," the wife may say. "He keeps doing it. He keeps hurting me."

"Well, keep forgiving him," I suggest.

Exasperated with the simplicity of my approach, she may open fire on me. That's when I know there is more to this than meets the eye. When a wife or husband will turn on the counselor, that's generally a good indicator that somebody is angry with someone who is not in the room. Free-floating anger, anger that can easily spill over on anyone in the vicinity, most often has it roots in a previous relationship.

Upon further investigation we usually discover that there are some unhealed wounds from the past—open wounds that the angry person's spouse keeps bumping up against. Wounds that are so painful that the wounded party has little choice but to protect and guard them. Often I find that the anger in the relationship was never even intended for the spouse. The spouse simply got in the way of anger that was directed at someone else. Someone from the past. Someone who had caused a wound that had never been nursed and healed.

People who are protecting wounds always lean toward self-centeredness. Self-centeredness limits an individual's potential for giving and receiving love. So there is conflict. And once again, a forgiveness issue becomes a character issue.

Different people handle hurt in different ways. Personally, I am prone to sitting around and having imaginary conversations with the people I am angry with. Imaginary conversations give me a feeling of power. I not only get to carefully choose my wording, I also get to make sure the other person sets me up for what I want to say. I always look good. In my imaginary conversations, there is always an audience present to watch me rip my enemy apart. And when I deliver that verbal death blow, everyone listening in is in full agreement. It's a wonderful pastime—or so I'm tempted to think.

But the whole system is fraught with lies. To begin with, it's not my responsibility to publicly humiliate my enemies. I am supposed to love them. Second, the perfect conversation with the perfect one-liners and stinging comebacks really wouldn't do that much for me. It wouldn't relieve me of my anger. Once the whole thing was said and done, I would feel the same way. Ripping someone apart verbally doesn't get me paid back. The debt will still be there. I may feel better temporarily for having unloaded on that person. But he still owes me. She still owes me. And I'm still angry.

Some seek satisfaction through sharing their story with others. They look for affirmation to help ease the pain. They just want to know that the world agrees that they were the victim. Some people will use just about any opportunity to tell their story. Maybe you've attended a small-group meeting where participants share prayer requests. And it seems like there's always one person who can't wait to unburden herself with a personal story. She's been hurt. She's angry. And she wants justice. And next week, she will feel the same way and share the same story. Because sharing does nothing to take away the debt.

## "SEVENTY TIMES SEVEN"

The other avenue for dealing with pain is to stuff it. We've all been told, "You shouldn't feel that way." As a result, a lot of Christians simply take their emotions and stuff them deep inside. They deny them all away.

This approach generally leads to depression. Depression is almost always caused by suppressed anger. Coping with anger by suppressing it only leads to other problems—problems that surface in the form of character deficiencies. It is difficult to be depressed and exercise self-control. It is nearly impossible for a depressed person to be gentle and kind. Depression leads to self-centered behavior, and understandably so. Depressed people are in pain. Whatever the reason, depression—suppressed anger—takes its toll on a person's character.

I don't know how Peter was accustomed to dealing with his hurts. I don't picture him as the type to suppress his feelings. And he certainly didn't act depressed. Whatever the case, he was ready to draw the line with someone and he wanted to know where the line was. "How many times shall I forgive my brother?" he asked.

Jesus said to him, "I tell you, not seven times, but seventy-seven times" (Matthew 18:22, NIV). And before Peter could respond, Jesus continued by telling one of the most intriguing parables in the New Testament:

"Therefore, the kingdom of heaven is like a king who wanted to settle accounts with his servants. As he began the settlement, a man who owed him ten thousand talents was brought to him. Since he was not able to pay, the master ordered that he and his wife and his children and all that he had be sold to repay the debt.

"The servant fell on his knees before him. 'Be patient with me,' he begged, 'and I will pay back everything.' The servant's master took pity on him, canceled the debt and let him go.

"But when the servant went out, he found one of his fellow servants who owed him a hundred denarii. He grabbed him and began to choke him. 'Pay back what you owe me!' he demanded.

"His fellow servant fell to his knees and begged him, 'Be patient with me, and I will pay you back.'

"But he refused. Instead, he went off and had the man thrown into prison until he could pay the debt. When the other servants saw what had happened, they were greatly distressed and went and told master everything that had happened.

"Then the master called the servant in. 'You wicked servant,' he said, 'I canceled all that debt of yours because you begged me to. Shouldn't you have had mercy on your fellow servant just as I had on you?' In anger his master turned him over to the jailers to be tortured, until he should pay back all he owed.

"This is how my heavenly Father will treat each of you unless you forgive your brother from your heart."

MATTHEW 18:32–35, NIV

Imagine how Peter must have felt as he listened to this story. In all likelihood he was looking for an excuse not to forgive. He wanted to draw a line and then exact justice himself. But as Jesus spoke, it was obvious that He was headed in a different direction.

As the parable unfolds, it becomes clear that God is the king. And wouldn't you know it, Peter is the wicked servant! After all, Peter had been forgiven of a great deal, and now he is demanding payment from his own offender! And then Jesus ends the parable with a stern warning: "This is how my heavenly Father will treat each of you unless you forgive your brother from your heart." Paraphrased, "If you don't forgive, God is coming after you."

At that point, Peter was probably sorry he ever asked the question. What a terrible thing to tell someone who is a victim. Peter must have been thinking, *Wait a minute! I've already been hurt once. I'm the victim. And now You're telling me that if I don't grant this person forgiveness—which he doesn't deserve—then God's coming after me, too?*

I'm not the most sensitive person in the world, but there is no way I would ever tell a hurting man or woman, "Look, you'd better forgive or God is coming after you!" Jesus' conclusion seems almost cruel. Those are tough words. And I tend to wonder right along with you, "Lord, how can You say that? I already have one enemy. I don't need You threatening me, too."

But our heavenly Father *demands* that we grant forgiveness. He even goes so far as to threaten us. And our negative response to that kind of language demonstrates our naïveté concerning the immense destructive force of bitterness and resentment.

As a father, I issue my most stern warnings when dealing with things that have the potential to harm my children. When I tell my two-year-old to get out of the street, I don't speak in a calm, warm, inviting tone of voice. I'm sure I sound somewhat threatening on those occasions. But I'm not mad. I'm not displeased. My tone of voice is influenced by two things: my love for my son and my knowledge of cars.

When Jesus addressed the issue of forgiveness, two things influenced the tone of His parable: His love for His children and His knowledge of bitterness. His warning is severe because the consequences of ignoring it are severe. Anger is nothing to mess around with. It is nothing to hold onto any longer than we have to. It is not a trophy to show off. It is not a story to tell. It is poison to our soul. To refuse to forgive is to choose to self-destruct.

## STEPS TO FORGIVENESS

Three things must take place for forgiveness to be complete. I hesitate to call them *steps*. They are more like processes—three processes necessary for the forgiveness cycle to be complete.

### Process #1: Charging the Defendant

If you have been hurt, something has been taken from you. To forgive, you must first identify exactly what has been taken or withheld. This is where most of us fail. We know we were wronged, but we never quite put our finger on what we expect in return. We fail to specifically identify exactly what was taken from us. We know what the person did, but we don't know exactly what the person took.

When we don't identify what has been taken, we go through the motions of forgiveness but experience no release. I've heard it a thousand times: "But I've already forgiven him!" Usually, that phrase is spoken with such intense energy that it's obvious forgiveness has not really taken place! General forgiveness does not heal specific hurts. It is important to pinpoint what was taken.

Maybe you've been blamed for something you didn't do. In that case, someone took your good reputation or robbed you of a promotion or potential relationship. Perhaps your father left you when you were a child. In that case, he robbed you of the experience of growing up with a dad who was there for you.

As Jesus illustrated in the parable, forgiveness revolves around canceling debts. Debt cancellation is at the heart of forgiveness, but you can't completely cancel a debt you have not thoroughly identified. This is one of the primary reasons people say prayers of forgiveness but continue to carry their anger.

### Process #2: Dropping the Charges

After identifying exactly what has been taken, you must then cancel the debt. That means proclaiming that the offending person doesn't owe you anything anymore. Instead of pressing charges, you simply drop the case. Just as Christ canceled your sin debt at Calvary, so you and I must cancel the sin debts that others have incurred against us. It's as simple as saying this:

> Heavenly Father, _____ has taken _____ from me. I have held on to this debt long enough. I choose to cancel this debt. _____ doesn't owe me anymore. Just as You forgave me, I forgive _____.

Please remember that forgiveness is not a feeling. It's a *decision.* You simply choose to cancel the debt. It's not something you have to share with the person who hurt you. And in most cases, to do so would be inappropriate. This is something between you and the Father.

It's tempting, of course, to judge whether or not we have forgiven by how we *feel* toward our offender. But our feelings toward someone are not always an accurate gauge; in fact, feelings are generally the last thing to come around. But in time, if you cling to the fact that this individual doesn't owe you anymore, even your feelings will change. The day will come when you will be able to respond to your offender in light of where he or she stands in relationship to the Father, rather than in light of how that person treated you.

## Process #3: Dismissing the Case

The final process centers on the daily decision not to reopen your case. What makes this so difficult is that our feelings don't automatically follow our decision to forgive. Besides that, forgiving someone doesn't erase our memory. If we could forgive and forget, this whole thing would be a lot easier. But in most cases, no sooner have we forgiven than something happens to remind us of the offense all over again. And when the memories recur, the old feelings recur as well.

One of two things usually happens at this juncture. We either take hold of the offense all over again, crank up the imaginary conversations, and reopen our case, or we try not to think about it. We try to turn our thoughts elsewhere. I may surprise you by saying that neither response is appropriate.

When memories of past hurt flood your mind, *go ahead and face them.* Allow yourself to remember the incident. It's even okay to feel the emotions those memories elicit. If necessary, be angry but do not sin (see Ephesians 4:26). But instead of reopening the case against your offender, instead of rehearsing images of retribution and revenge, use it as an opportunity to renew your mind.

Pinpoint once again the thing you were robbed of. Then thank your heavenly Father for giving you the grace and strength to forgive. Thank Him as well for forgiving you. Don't accept the lie that you haven't really forgiven. Focus on the truth. The truth is, you have decided to cancel the debt, and so the debt has been canceled. How do you know? Because you decided, as an act of your will, to cancel it.

Our memories are not enemies of forgiveness. Memories are simply memories. What we do with them determines their impact. Our memories are opportunities to renew our minds to what we know is true. Our memories are opportunities to rejoice in our own forgiveness. Truly forgiving does not always entail truly forgetting. If you will renew your mind, painful memories can become reminders of God's goodness and grace and healing power in your life. What were once negative memories can become a source of joy as you experience the healing power of the Father.

Forgiveness is the avenue for the most significant expressions of character. It paves the way for us to love our enemies and pray for those who have persecuted us. Forgiveness is a nonnegotiable in our pursuit of character.

# Chapter Thirteen

# LEARNING TO WALK AGAIN

*For when I am weak, then I am strong.*
2 CORINTHIANS 12:10

T he story is told of an old farmer who was struggling to keep pace with the newer high-tech farms in his area. A staunch believer in doing things the old-fashioned way, he considered the newfangled shortcuts of horticultural engineering to be a passing fad. Creating hearty hybrid plants and using the latest fertilizing techniques, the new farms were doubling and tripling their previous crop yields. The old farmer needed a plan to compete. But rather than take advantage of the new technology, he set out to beat it single-handedly.

His solution was simple.

He would clear a large, wooded section of his land and convert it into plowable fields. There was just one problem. Cutting all those trees would take months. And he would never get the land cleared in time for planting season. "If only I could come up with a faster way to cut trees," he pondered.

As luck would have it, the old farmer stumbled across an advertisement in a magazine. It featured a new chainsaw that promised to cut through a twenty-inch log in twenty seconds. "One inch per second!" he thought. At that rate, he could clear his entire property in time for planting season. It was exactly what he'd been looking for. So he hurried to the general store and purchased the new saw.

The old farmer set out early the next morning to begin expanding his farmland. Eagerly, he selected a twenty-inch oak tree as his first victim. With great anticipation, he set the cutting chain against the trunk of the tree and went to work. Twenty seconds passed and the tree remained standing. He continued on, reasoning that it was his first attempt and that he would get the hang of it gradually. After five minutes, with the tree still towering over him, he began to wonder if he was doing something wrong. And when a full hour had passed with only a small cut in the side of the tree to show for it, the farmer packed up the saw and headed back to the general store.

The clerk listened patiently as the old farmer explained his lack of progress and ranted about the great promises stated in the advertisement. "Let's take a look at it," the clerk suggested. With his left hand gripping the handle, the clerk braced the saw against the front porch of the general store. Then, taking his right hand, he grabbed the rubber handle on the side of the saw and gave a quick pull. Instantly, the saw roared to life. Startled, the old farmer jumped back several feet and exclaimed, "What's that noise!?"

## STRENGTH FOR THE JOURNEY

The concepts in this book may have caught your attention as that magazine ad did for the old farmer. *This is what I've been looking for,* you told yourself. And if you have read this far, it's quite possible that these pages have motivated and even equipped you to make the development of your character a real priority.

But like the old farmer, there is something you may not know. And I would be less than honest not to mention it in closing: *In and of yourself, you don't have what it takes to become a man or woman of character.*

You can't do it.

Not on your own, anyway.

Sooner or later you'll discover that all the motivation in the world, by itself, is not enough to carry you across the finish line. All the principles, maxims, and strategies aren't enough. In addition to those things, you need power. You need enablement. You need help. What God has begun in you, only He can complete. You not only need His plan to direct you, you need His strength to empower you.

You cannot change yourself any more than you could save yourself! You cannot transform your character in your own strength. Real change involves revelations about ourselves that we will never make on our own. Change requires renewal. And renewal requires the excavating work of the Holy Spirit. Jesus referred to Him as the Spirit of truth (John 15:26). Ultimately, it is the Holy Spirit that shines the light of God's truth into the dark places of our hearts.

To become a person of character, you need the enabling power of the Holy Spirit.

Living in your own strength is like pushing a car instead of driving it. Yes, there is progress. But it is slow, inconsistent, and extremely inefficient. As long as you are pushing your car, there are places you can't go, hills you can't climb, vistas you'll never reach. And at times, it takes every bit of strength you have just to keep from losing ground. As long as you are pushing your car, there is no joy and no sense of satisfaction. It's certainly not something you look forward to.

Pursuing character in your own strength can be an equally frustrating and joyless endeavor. Progress is slow. It's possible to spend years of your life just holding your own. And when you let up, even for a moment, the gravitational forces of society have the power to pull you back down to where you started. After a few years of that approach, even the *thought* of pursuing Christlike character can make you tired. Why bother? It's too exhausting. The progress-to-effort ratio makes it a bad investment of your time and energy.

There's one other thing about pushing your car. The stronger you are, the farther you can push it. The stronger you are, the longer you can go before you deplete your physical reserves and start looking for alternatives. In the same way, it takes some believers longer than others to come to the end of themselves. It takes some longer than others to throw up their hands in frustration and say, "God, I can't do this! If anything is going to happen, You're going to have to get involved in a far more evident way."

As Christians, we operate in one of two modes—our strength or God's. Needless to say, there's an unimaginably great difference between the two. Most believers readily agree that they have needed God's strength to get them through some trying times in their lives. They agree that there are certain temptations and trials they cannot overcome without help from above. It's not uncommon to hear a Christian ask God to provide strength for the challenges of the day.

But for many, this is only rhetoric. These are just nice things to say. Confessing one's dependency upon God communicates a sense of humility and spirituality. Yet oftentimes there is no spiritual reality behind the words. No real sense of dependence. Instead there is sincere, but insufficient, self-effort. And eventually, there is a deep, abiding frustration.

These two sources of strength result in two contrasting approaches to the Christian life—the *religious* approach and the *relational* approach. The religious approach centers on our ability to do for God and His corresponding obligation to do for us. The relational approach centers on what God has done for us and what He is willing to do through us.

## THE RELIGIOUS APPROACH

If you think about it, there's something appealing about the religious approach. On the surface it seems fair. We do something for God, and He does something for us in return. What could be fairer than that? It feels right. After all, the harder a person works, the better off he or she ought to be. Hard work should be rewarded.

As believers, we are usually quick to reject the notion of salvation by works. And rightly so. The Gospels are clear: Salvation comes through faith in Christ. Our belief in salvation by faith is what sets us apart from other religions in this world. And yet once we move beyond our salvation experience, we are prone to begin approaching life religiously. That is, we measure our approval and acceptance rating with God according to our deeds. Good deeds equal approval. Bad deeds—sins—equal rejection.

If the truth were known, most of the people who will go to church this weekend will do so out of a sense of obligation. It's one of those "ought to" kinds of things. At an emotional level, they believe they will be in better standing with God for going. And if they don't go, they feel as if it might be held against them.

Most of us get caught up in this sort of thinking from time to time. We believe deep down that if we're going to have any kind of connection with God, that connection is dependent on some sort of routine, some sort of ritual, some sort of scoring system. But nothing could be further from the truth. And nothing could be more counterproductive to our pursuit of character. Why? Because religion and self-effort go hand in hand.

Find me a man or woman who is attempting to win God's approval through good works, and I will show you a person who is operating from his or her own limited strength. As long as we view our deeds as a bridge to intimacy with and approval from God, we are depending upon our strength. God does not empower us to win His approval. We have all the approval we could ever need! Approval and acceptance were settled at Calvary. Christ won the Father's approval for us by removing the barrier of sin. Approval is a gift to be accepted, not a wage to be earned.

The Bible has a name for the "earn your way" approach to God. It's called *walking according to the flesh.* It's a self-protecting, look-out-for-number-one, what's-in-it-for-me approach to life. The strange thing about it is that a person walking according to the flesh can be in church one minute (when that serves his purposes) and be in bed with his neighbor's wife the next.

The flesh takes its cue from the needs and desires of a man. So when an individual who is walking according to the flesh senses a need for religion, the flesh will seek out religion; when that same individual longs for inappropriate companionship, the flesh can accommodate that as well.

## THE RELATIONAL APPROACH

Whereas the religious approach leaves us to do our best in our own strength, the relational approach to Christianity involves a new source of strength and an ability to do what was formerly impossible to do. The best way to get a handle on the relational approach is to think through what happens when a person becomes a Christian.

Salvation involves putting our trust in what Christ did in *His* strength on the cross. When we put our faith in Him, He did something for us we could not possibly do on our own: He removed the barrier of sin. He took away the penalty of our sin that was looming over us. Our part was simply to believe and receive. We believed His promise and received His life. It was an effortless transaction from our standpoint.

Now with all that in mind, think about the implications of this verse: "As you therefore have received Christ Jesus the Lord, so walk in Him" (Colossians 2:6, NKJV).

The attitude and perspective we had at the moment of our salvation is to be the attitude and perspective we maintain in our daily walk with God. You accepted Christ as Savior because you were unable to save yourself. In effect, you said, "I cannot; You can." Then you trusted Him to do what you could not do. And through His power, you were saved by grace through faith (see Ephesians 2:8–9).

God never intended for us to shift out of the *I can't, You can* way of thinking. What was necessary for becoming a Christian is equally necessary for living as a Christian. The perspective we had at the moment of our salvation is meant to be the perspective we maintain throughout our Christian experience. We did not have the strength to save ourselves from the penalty of sin. Neither do we have the power to save ourselves from our daily encounters with the power of sin.

The childlikeness that realized, "I need You. I'm powerless. I can't do it without You," was intended as the attitude we were to maintain throughout our lives. But old ways don't die easily. And so most of us went right back to relating to God through rituals, rules, and tradition. Granted, some of the rules were different after our salvation. And there were several new traditions we had to get accustomed to. But our approach was the same: "God, I'll do my best to obey You."

As we grew in knowledge, most of us were willing to accept the fact that God had an absolute system of right and wrong to which we were accountable. Our problems started when we realized we didn't have the will to follow through.

## THE EMPOWERED WILL

A man or woman of character is someone who has the will to do what is right. Not just the desire, but the will. That is, they have the ability, the power, and the strength to follow through. And please keep this in mind: When we talk about character, we aren't talking about "being nice." We are talking about the very character of Christ Himself.

The truth is, in our own strength, we don't have the will to follow through. Only one person's will is up to that monumental challenge—the will of Him whose character we seek. Only one person can consistently manifest the character of Christ, and that one person is Christ Himself. Consequently, the *power of Christ* is necessary to manifest the *character of Christ*. And that power is available to us only through the Holy Spirit.

The pursuit of character entails surrender to and dependency upon the Holy Spirit. The biblical terminology for this approach to life is *walking according to the Spirit*. Think for a moment about the cause-and-effect dynamic of this verse:

> But I say, walk by the Spirit, and you will not carry out the desire
> of the flesh.
>
> GALATIANS 5:16

The desires of the flesh—desires that conflict with the character we seek—can be overcome by means of walking by the Spirit. This verse is actually a promise. If we walk by the Spirit, we will not fulfill the desires of the flesh. We will be empowered to choose the path of character. We will be strengthened to *will* to do the right thing.

Here's another way to look at it. As you consider those elements you would like to develop within your character over the coming months and years, do any of them resemble such qualities as love, joy, peace, patience, kindness, goodness, faithfulness, gentleness, and self-control? Chances are, they do. This is a list of characteristics and virtues that the Holy Spirit desires to produce through us (see Galatians 5:22–23).

The apostle Paul refers to them as the fruits of the Spirit because they are produced *by the Spirit.* These are not qualities we can produce on our own, in our own strength. These are not virtues we are commanded to go out and attain on our own. These are characteristics the heavenly Father longs to produce through His children as they learn to rely upon and draw upon His strength. Character is produced through us; it is not manufactured by us.

The flesh is fueled by self-effort. And self-effort is insufficient for the kind of changes we are talking about. Self-effort cannot consistently drum up what it takes to *will* to do what is right. And so the whole process breaks down. Good intentions, determination, preparation, strategies—none of these things are powerful enough to overcome the power of the flesh. Only the Holy Spirit can enable a believer to will to do what is right, regardless of the cost.

The problem is not that you're not dedicated enough. The problem is not that you haven't tried hard enough. The problem is that what you are attempting to accomplish is impossible in your own strength. And so God sent His Spirit to lead and empower us. The whole thing is intensely relational.

## WALKING IN RELATIONSHIP

Walking according to the Spirit is purely a relational endeavor. It begins with surrender. Surrender to a person. Surrender to His standard and will for your life. Walking in the Spirit can be defined like this: Moment-by-moment dependence upon the Holy Spirit to prompt you to do what He wants you to do, and to empower you to do what you cannot do. Notice that this approach doesn't compromise God's standards. It's not a license to sin. The goal is still the same: the character of Christ. It's just that the method of getting there is different.

Certainly, there are rules. But the rules are intended to give us a picture of where God is taking us. They foreshadow what we'll look like as God gradually transforms us into the image of Christ. Our job is not to keep rules. Our job is to walk in the Spirit. Because if we walk in the Spirit, then we will not fulfill the desires of the flesh. That's the path to character.

Just as you relied on God to free you from the *penalty* of sin, you must now rely on God to free you from the *power* of sin. Your spirit is set free from the penalty of sin—eternal death—at the point of salvation. But as long as you remain on this earth, your earthly body will continue to be the target of sin's temptation and destructive power. Your pursuit of Christ's character hinges on your day-to-day dependence on the power of His Holy Spirit to empower you toward Christlikeness.

Your primary goal should be to live in an ongoing state of surrender, acknowledging that without the intervention of the Holy Spirit you will be defeated by the power of sin. If there is a singular theme that emerges from the entirety of Scripture, it is this: Through relationship with God, man is finally capable of doing that which he was incapable of doing on his own. That's what walking in the Spirit is all about.

And that's what character is all about.

## FOLLOW THE LEADER

You are dependent upon your heavenly Father. I am dependent. We need to recognize our dependency and act on it. We ought to declare our dependency every morning when we rise. And we ought to thank Him for His sufficiency every evening as we close our eyes to sleep. Character is the by-product of dependency. For when we are weak, then He is strong. And when we allow Him to be strong in us, He produces His fruit through us.

If I were to invite you to my house, there are several ways I could get you there. To begin with, I could give you a map. I could say, "Here's what you do: You get on GA 400 and go north. Take exit 9 and go left. Once you exit, just follow this map. I'll see you at my house."

If you followed the directions on the map, eventually you would arrive at my house. With this approach, you could measure your success according to your ability to read a map and follow the directions. Thanks to my map and your ability to follow it, all would be well.

That's a picture of walking according to the flesh. You've got your instructions, you've got your list, and you measure your success by your ability to execute—to do what's right. But notice where your focus is: It's on the map. And your relationship with the Father is not front and center in your thinking. Instead, it is a list of dos and don'ts.

If God had intended us to follow a list, He would have said, "Here's a map. Do the best you can, and I'll see you at My house." But He didn't. He said, "I have come that they may have life, and have it to the full" (John 10:10, NIV) and "I am with you always" (Matthew 28:20, NIV). He's not just interested in your destination. He's interested in your journey as well.

The other way I could get you to my house is to say, "Get in your car, I'll pull around, and you can follow me."

You might respond, "But which way are we going?"

"Just follow me."

"Are we going to get on the interstate?"

"Just follow me."

"Which exit will we take?"

"*Just follow me.* I won't lose you or leave you behind."

And so our journey would begin. When I turned left, you would turn left. When I turned right, you would turn right. And eventually you would arrive at my house. You would arrive at the same place, by the same route, in approximately the same amount of time as you would have by following the map. But instead of focusing on a map, your focus would have been on me. Moment by moment, mile by mile, you would be dependent upon me. I would have had your undivided attention.

God's goal for you isn't just to end up at the right place. His goal is relationship. The goal is constant dependence upon His Spirit—dependence for direction and dependence for the strength to follow through. And when that becomes your approach to life, you will not only get to the right place, you'll get there the right way. And along the way, you'll know Him. And in knowing Him you will discover His character. The very character He longs to recreate in you.

## THE DECISION TO FOLLOW

Of course, there's another way I could get you to my house. I could put you in the car and drive you there. And for years, I thought that was the picture of walking in the Spirit. I thought, *I'm going to grow and grow, and I'm probably going to become so committed, so surrendered, so rededicated that one day God will finally say, "Andy, you've finally reached the priestly plateau...the angelic echelon...the holy hierarchy! From here on out, it's an easy ride."*

I thought walking in the Spirit was a level we reached after years of listening to tapes, reading books, having marathon quiet times, and going further and further into the deeper things of God. I assumed there was a point out there somewhere when the Christian life would get easier. I was hoping for an infusion of willpower that would make choosing to sin out of the question.

I would hear sermons about "letting go and letting God." And I'd keep letting go and letting go and waiting for God to scoop me up and change me. But that's not what it means to walk in the Spirit. Because at some point in that little transfer, God would have to infringe upon your power to choose. And once He did that, the significance and authenticity of your worship and allegiance would be diminished. Freedom to choose is a prerequisite for a genuine relationship.

Still, don't you sometimes wish God would take control of your mind? Wouldn't it be easier if we could walk down an aisle, pray a prayer, push a button, and suddenly God would take over? As attractive as that may sound at times, God doesn't want to control you. If control was His goal, He could have accomplished that long before now. Relationship is His goal. And to make that possible, He has given us the gift of freedom. Freedom to choose. Freedom to follow. Freedom to surrender.

As we follow, surrendered to His will and purposes, He empowers us to follow through on what He desires for us to do. Surrender is a sign of weakness. And where and when we are weak, He is strong. Our salvation didn't begin with a commitment to something. It started with dependence on Somebody. And the day-to-day Christian life is the same way. It's not about committing to something. It's about depending upon Someone.

## BABY STEPS

When my son Andrew first started to walk, we played out a scene in our house that's played out in virtually every household that has children. You've probably witnessed the scene yourself. Here's our precious little angel who's been crawling around for months. And finally he starts pulling himself up and standing on those little legs. He's standing there, holding onto the arm of a chair with one hand, looking like he's ready to let go. He has that big, goofy grin on his face, a little drool on his chin, and one leg in the air.

Then the big moment comes. He attempts his first step. And there we are, camcorder in hand, cheering and encouraging him, "Come on, come on!" Of course, Andrew doen't even know what's going on. I've got my arms stretched out in his direction and a big, goofy grin on my face as well. And suddenly—false alarm. He wraps both arms around the arm of the chair and just stands there, giggling.

So we do what every parent does at that point. We start bribing him. We hold out toys, food, whatever we can get our hands on that will make him want to move in our direction. And then it happens. Andrew looks at Sandra, glances at me, and then locks in on the bribe. His eyes grow wide with excitement. Then he drops to his knees and crawls just as fast as he can to receive his reward.

And then the whole process begins again. And once again, Andrew drops to his knees and crawls. Now why do you suppose Andrew keeps acting that way? That's easy. Because crawling comes naturally to a baby. It's what they do. It's what he's been doing since the day he became mobile. It's all he knows.

Living life in our strength comes naturally to us as well. We have an internal propensity for independence. Approaching life from the standpoint of weakness rather than strength seems foreign, awkward. So when the pressure's on, when we see something we really want—even something as beneficial as character—we drop to our hands and knees and begin to crawl.

But you were designed to walk in the Spirit, not crawl through life in your own strength. Learning to walk, physically or spiritually, takes time. It is a process. It begins with baby steps. It involves a series of setbacks in which we revert to our old ways of coping. And as is the case with children, to refuse to learn is to choose to be handicapped for life.

## FIRST STEP

For you, that first baby step may mean getting up tomorrow morning and simply saying, "Lord Jesus, today I cannot. But You can." Rehearse your day with Him. Pray through your schedule, claiming victory over the temptations you generally face. Think through the stressful moments you are anticipating. For the most part, you can predict those circumstances that will test your character. Go ahead and claim your dependency ahead of time. As you imagine yourself moving through the paces of the day, tell the Lord, "I cannot; You can."

> "Lord, I'll probably run into _____. You know how difficult it is for me not to gossip when I'm around her. I have a difficult time keeping my mouth shut. I cannot, but You can."

> "Father, today I want to honor my husband. But You know how difficult that is for me right now. I cannot, Lord. But You can."

> "Today I have to give _____ an answer. I know what You want me to say. But I don't have the strength to say, 'No.' I cannot, but You can."

"Today I will see _____. Lord, I cannot control my thoughts when she is around. I cannot, but You can."

"This is going to be a stressful day. Father, You know I have a tendency to lose my cool when the pressure is on. I confess that I cannot handle the events of this day, but You can. Handle them through me."

Your pursuit of character was not intended to be a solo flight. It is not about doing your best or being all you can be. No doubt, you have tried being all you can be. And like so many, you have discovered that "all you can be" isn't going to cut it. We need to be what we aren't, and on our own, we can't become anything other than what we are.

For this reason, God sent the Holy Spirit to live inside of you. He came to direct and empower you. He will enable you to be what in your own strength you could never be: a person of character. When you can't, He can. His optimum working environment is your weakness. His primary tool is truth. His final product is a reproduction of the character of Christ in you.

So pull out your list of character goals and write across the top in big letters, "I CANNOT, BUT YOU CAN." Declare your weakness. Reaffirm your dependence. And ask your heavenly Father to teach you what it means to walk according to the Spirit.

For when you are weak, He is strong.

# Chapter Fourteen

# THE FINISH LINE

The crowd roared with excitement as the lead runner came into view. His name was German Silva. And with only seven hundred yards between him and victory, he was beginning to feel the exhilaration of the moment.

The 1994 edition of the prestigious New York City Marathon had become the object of more media attention than any previous race. This was the event's silver anniversary. The race featured a reunion of the inaugural runners, and an air show was scheduled to cap off the celebration. And now the circus of events surrounding the marathon paused as the eyes of New York focused on the climactic finish of the race.

Silva had run almost twenty-six miles. But that distance didn't begin to describe the route he had traveled to get here. This was the fulfillment of a dream that was born in a tiny, impoverished village in rural Mexico.

Back home, his mother waited anxiously for word of his success. Back home, there was no sports coverage on television. Back home, there wasn't even electricity. For nearly all of his twenty-six years, it seemed Silva had been running toward the dream of something better for his mother, his people, and his village. And as he passed through the tunnel of blurred faces, colorful banners, and screaming fans, he felt closer than ever to the finish line.

Trailing close behind was his friend and frequent training partner, Benjamin Paredes. Together, they had assumed control of the race at the twenty-three-mile mark. Stride for stride, they matched each other through Central Park. By all appearances, the most celebrated New York City Marathon in history was about to see the event's most exciting conclusion ever.

Silva remained confident. Having trained with Paredes, he knew that he held the upper hand. If it came down to a sprint, Silva was the faster runner. And as he neared the final stretch, he began to ease ahead of his fellow countryman. Just ahead of him, the camera car set the pace as the production crew captured the dramatic climax of the race and piped it into the homes of millions of spectators around the world. Physically and mentally exhausted, Silva focused on the back of the vehicle and steadily increased his lead.

With only a few hundred yards to go, the car left Central Park South and made a right turn into the Seventh Avenue entrance of the park. With impenetrable focus, Silva followed close behind. He was no longer aware of his teammate's presence behind him. His lead seemed secure. But as the cheers of the crowd suddenly turned from celebration to alarm, Silva could sense that something was wrong.

When he glanced up at the faces along the route, they seemed painfully distressed. A policeman flailed his arms wildly, pointing back in the direction of Central Park South. Suddenly Silva realized that he was going the wrong way. The car he was following had turned off the course in order to clear the path to the finish line. And by the time he got turned around, Silva had given his friend a fifty-yard advantage.

Silva made a feverish sprint for the finish. With less than two-tenths of a mile to go, Silva somehow managed to catch up with Paredes. And as the two crossed the finish line, Silva emerged with the smallest lead in the marathon's history, beating his teammate by less than two seconds.

When it was over, Silva dedicated his effort to his father, Abigato, who turned seventy the next day. "Before, he didn't want me to become a runner because the situation in my village was very hard," said Silva upon accepting the spoils of $150,000 and a new Mercedes. "Now, I think he's one of my biggest fans."[6]

## A NARROW ESCAPE

German Silva narrowly escaped one of the greatest sporting disasters of our time. He was physically superior to his opponents, he was well prepared for the race, and he was mentally focused. For a few critical seconds, however, he channeled all his talent and years of training in the wrong direction. And it almost cost him the race.

Life is a race. Everybody runs. But it is not enough to run hard. You've got to run in the right direction. That means taking time to answer questions like these:

1. What is success for me?
2. What do I want to become?
3. What do I want to be remembered for?

God may have blessed you with all the talent in the world. You may have a great education. You may be surrounded with wonderful opportunities. But unless you take time to discover what's really important to you, until you define your personal finish line, you could find yourself winning a race you never intended to run. Years down the road, you may be looking back at a life fully invested in a commodity that did not pay the kind of return you were looking for.

Your heavenly Father wants to create in you the very character of the Savior. His desire is to conform you to the image of His son. But this is a process—a process in which God Himself takes a personal interest. And it is a process in which you play an important role.

God is working to shape and form you from the inside out. And as you align your will with His, change *will* take place.

Change that will prepare you for the inevitable storms of life.

Change that will give you influence with those who are watching.

Change that will reflect well on your heavenly Father.

Change that will result in a life that speaks louder than words.

The publisher and author would love to hear your comments about this book. *Please contact us at:* www.multnomah.net/andystanley

# NOTES

1. James M. Kouzes and Barry Z. Posner, *The Leadership Challenge* (San Francisco: Jossey Bass Publishers, 1987), 16.

2. C. S. Lewis, *The Case for Christianity* (New York: Macmillan, 1943), 5.

3. Bill McCartney, *Ashes to Glory* (Nashville, TN: Thomas Nelson, 1995).

4. Larry Crabb, *Men and Women: Enjoying the Differences* (Grand Rapids, MI: Zondervan, 1993).

5. Samuel Nisenson and William A. DeWitt, *Illustrated Minute Biographies* (New York: Grosset & Dunlap, 1964).

6. *NY Running News,* January/December 1995.

# Look for More Great Titles
## *from Andy Stanley*

### THE BEST QUESTION EVER
Asking this question at the right moment holds the key to experiencing a full life without regrets. The answer to this question will shed light on life's gray areas and clear the fog away from difficult decisions involving relationships, career, finances, family and health.
**ISBN 1-59052-390-3**

### 7 PRACTICES OF EFFECTIVE MINISTRY
An engaging parable about one overwhelmed pastor is followed by an overview of seven team practices, developed and successfully applied in a ministry setting. These clear, easy, and strategic practices can turn your organization into a winning team.
**ISBN 1-59052-378-4**

### DISCOVERING GOD'S WILL
God has a personal vision for each of our lives and He wants us to know it. Learn how you can effect lifelong personal change as you pursue His vision for your life.
**ISBN 1-59052-379-2**

### PARENTAL GUIDANCE REQUIRED
Your children's life experiences and decisions will be greatly impacted by the quality of their relationships. Learn how you can enhance your relationship with your children, influence their relationships outside the home, and to advance their relationship with God.
**ISBN 1-59052-381-4**

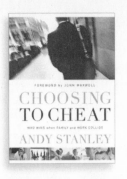

### CHOOSING TO CHEAT
Let's face it. You just can't fit everything in. Decide what commitments you can cheat on—and how to truly please God with your twenty-four hours.

**ISBN 1-59052-329-6**

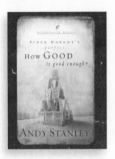

### HOW GOOD IS GOOD ENOUGH?
Goodness is not even a requirement to enter God's kingdom—thankfully, because we'll never be good enough. And Christianity is beyond fair—it's merciful.

**ISBN 1-59052-274-5**

### THE NEXT GENERATION LEADER
Be the kind of leader you'd admire! Find inspiration, encouragement, and proven advice from pastor and bestselling author Andy Stanley.

**ISBN 1-59052-046-7**

### VISIONEERING
Explore with Andy Stanley the ordinary life of Nehemiah and his vision for accomplishing the extraordinary. Discover the direction, motivation, and encouragement you need to know God's vision for what can be—and should be.

**ISBN 1-57673-787-X**